D1523795

The Scarecrow Author Bibliographies

WILLIAM EVERSON:
A Descriptive Bibliography
1934-1976

by
Lee Bartlett
and
Allan Campo

The Scarecrow Author Bibliographies, No. 33

The Scarecrow Press, Inc.
Metuchen, N.J. and London
1977

Library of Congress Cataloging in Publication Data

Bartlett, Lee, 1950-
    William Everson : a descriptive bibliography, 1934-
1976.

    (The Scarecrow author bibliographies ; no. 33)
    Includes index.
    1. Everson, William, 1912-   --Bibliography.
I. Campo, Allan, joint author.
Z8279.3.B37   [PS3509.V65]   016.811'5'2   77-5397
ISBN 0-8108-1037-9

for
James Laughlin
and
Robert Hawley

CONTENTS

PREFACE

The writing and publishing career of William Everson has spanned more than forty years and is certainly one of the most substantial and most interesting in modern literature. In his introductory essay for <u>The Achievement of Brother Antoninus</u>, William Stafford wrote of Everson that

> he has carried from farm to camp to home to monastery the accumulation of his work and even the means to print it. As he himself was a printer and as his friends were often engaged in writing and publishing, and as they often considered their work to be independent, outside the mainstream, his bibliography has become very much tangled. His writing and publishing make an elaborate puzzle, with partial printings of certain large works, and with consequent gaps in the material he considers continuous.

Stafford's statement appeared in 1967. Nine years since then, many of the gaps have been filled, yet the bibliography remains tangled. Here we have attempted to cut the Gordian Knot.

This bibliography is comprised of six sections, plus an appendix. Sections A and B are descriptive, based on the model used by Donald Gallup in his Pound bibliography. Section A lists all books, pamphlets, and broadsides by William Everson published between 1935 and 1976, and following some descriptions contains other information which is useful from a bibliographical standpoint. Section B lists those books which contain intro-

vii

ductions by the poet; some of these items, especially
the Robinson Jeffers material, have been edited by him
--others have not.

Gallup's descriptive method was used:

the general rule is that when the unnumbered
printed preliminary leaves count up (as pages)
to the first numbered page of the book, these
leaves are not specified in the collation. When
they do not count up, they are specified: e.g.
1 blank leaf, 3 leaves, 9-29 pp., because here
the printed preliminary material counts up to
only six pages. When the first numbered page
is the verso of a leaf unnumbered on the recto,
the number of the recto is supplied in square
brackets: e.g. 1 blank leaf, 3 leaves, (9)-29
pp., thus indicating that 10 is the first page
numbered. The collation '29 pp.' alone indicates that the preliminary material counts up
to the first numbered page and that the text
ends on a page numbered 29.... The collation
'29, (1) pp.', on the other hand, indicates
either that the text ends on the unnumbered
page (30), or that a colophon, index, or some
other printed material appears on that page.
'29 pp., 1 leaf' indicates that the text ends on
page 29 and that additional material not a con-
tinuation of the text appears on a final unnumbered leaf, either recto or verso or both being
printed. Because the collation accounts for all
leaves present in a complete copy of each book,
half-title-leaves have not been noted except
where the wording of the half-title-page differs
significantly from that of the title-page.

Sections C and D are checklists of Everson's
contributions to periodicals. Section C lists poetry,
while Section D lists and briefly annotates Everson's
essays, reviews, interviews, and letters. Section E
contains a list of anthologies in which the poet's work
has appeared. Section F lists and annotates selected
ephemera. Finally, a list of unpublished manuscripts

appears in the appendix, as well as a checklist of selected criticism. Lee Bartlett has compiled sections A and B; Allan Campo, sections C and D. The remainder of this bibliography has been a collaborative effort.

By way of acknowledgment, we would like to thank first of all William Everson for giving us access to his personal collection, as well as for his willingness to help at all turns with information regarding his career. Secondly, thanks go to Johan O. Johnson, Virginia C. West, Ruth Galvin Thornburg, Estelle Rebec and the Bancroft Library, Steve Eisner, and the staffs of the William Andrews Clark Memorial Library and the Department of Special Collections, Shields Library, University of California, Davis. We have made some use of David Kherdian's Six Poets of the San Francisco Renaissance (Fresno, 1967), which in turn made substantial use of an earlier checklist prepared by Allan Campo. Finally, a special thanks to Mary Dougherty for returning early from Guatemala so the work could be completed, and to Al Bartlett.

L. B. & A. C.

A. BOOKS, PAMPHLETS,
AND BROADSIDES
BY WILLIAM EVERSON

A1   THESE ARE THE RAVENS   1935

Pamphlet Series of Western Poets / These Are The
Ravens / [device] By [device] / Bill Everson / Price
10 Cents / Copyright 1935, By Bill Everson / Printed
in the United States of America / By Greater West Publishing Co. , San Leandro, Calif. / [in purple: decorative rules along left margin]

3-11 pp.   22 x 14. 5 cm.   Printed wrappers, stapled.

Published in 1935 in an edition of 1,000 copies by Greater West Publishing Company, San Leandro, California,
at 10 cents.   A long publisher's note is included on
verso of front wrapper.

Contains: "These Are the Ravens," "Winter Plowing,"
"Red Sky at Morning," "October Tragedy," "First Win-
ter Storm," "Over the Roads," "To an Indian-Hunting
Posse," "Who Lives Here Harbors Sorrow," "Martin's
Homestead," "Let It Be Told," "I Know It as the Sor-
row," "Tor House," "But There Was No Lament," "Do
Not Brood for Long," "Fog Days," "Muscat Pruning. "

Note: 15 copies of These Are the Ravens were specially
bound in orange wrappers by the poet.   Cover: These
Are The / Ravens / by / Bill Everson.   Colophon on
recto end cover reads: Fifteen copies speci- / ally covered by Bill / Everson at The Ever- / son Printery,
Novem- / ber 27, 1935 ... / This copy presented to.

A2   SAN JOAQUIN   1939

[in brown: design] / [in black: rule] / [in red: device]
[in black:] San Joaquin [device] By William Everson /
Printed By The Ward Ritchie Press / Los Angeles, California.   1939

xiv pp. , 1 leaf, 38 pp. , 1 leaf.   20. 7 x 15. 7 cm.   Brown
paper covered boards with illustration of grape vine on
stake on front and back.   Cloth backed spine, printed
brown paper pasted: [device] / San Joaquin / [device]
/ Everson / [device].   White end-papers, pages untrimmed.

Published in 1939 by the Ward Ritchie Press in an edition of 100 copies.   Title-page decoration drawn by Hu-
bert Buel.   Dedicated to Edwa Everson, with foreword
by Lawrence Clark Powell.   Copy inspected contains inscription: "for Kenneth, Aug. 7, 1939, Bill. "

Contains: "Fish-Eaters," "Fog," "Attila," "We in the
Fields," "Lines for the Last of a Gold Town," "August, "
"Who Sees Through the Lens," "Bard," "On the Anni-
versary of the Versailles Peace," "Winter Solstice, "
"Year's End," "San Joaquin," "The Rain on That Morn-
ing," "In the Shift of the Stars," "Circumstance," "The
Knives," "Sleep," "Elegy for a Ruined Schoolhouse, "
"Noon," "New Mexican Landscape," "Thunder," "We
Knew It for Autumn," "Love Song," "Spade," "Wind
West," "Winter Sundown," "Oh Fortunate Earth," "Ver-
nal Equinox," "Abrasive," "Coast Thought," "Sun, "
"Outside This Music," " Trifles," "House on Second
Street," "Walls," "Clouds. "

Note: A typescript at the William Andrews Clark Library
(Los Angeles) shows an earlier title, "The Blue Wind of
September. "

A3   THE MASCULINE DEAD   1942

The Masculine Dead / Poems, 1938-1940 / William
Everson / [device] / The Press of James A. Decker /
Prairie City, Illinois

5-44 pp.   22. 5 x 15. 2 cm.   Fabricord over boards.
Gold stamp on front cover: the / masculine / dead /
[device] / William Everson.

Published in 1942 by James Decker in an edition of
about 200 copies, at $2. 00.   According to David Kher-
dian, "The 100 copies received by the author as royalty
payment contain the publisher's errata slip which the
author tipped-on to face p. 44.   All of the copies received by the author were bound in green fabricord,
with lettering same as above, and without the errata
slip, which would indicate that all copies placed for sale
by the publisher were issued without an errata slip.
The one such copy inspected was bound in maroon fabricord. "

The compiler examined two presentation copies.   The
first, bound in green fabricord but containing no errata
slip, was given to Kenneth Carothers by the author.   It
contains corrections in the author's hand.   Inscription:
"for Kenny--with my personal corrections!--and with my
regret that what was so generously conceived should
have so wretched a fulfillment.   Bill Sept 24, 1942 Selma. "   A second inscription written on paper has been
taped-in below first inscription: "Kenny--the other books
are available and may be tossed about the barracks, but
this is rare, and should be guarded.   B. "   The second
presentation copy was given to Lee Watkins.   It contains an errata slip pasted before title page, and the following note: "Lee Watkins, donor of this book and
friend of William Everson, relates that at one time the
Press of James A Decker did very good work and that
Everson expected good work on this book.   He was very
disappointed in the results of this printing.   Before giving a copy to Watkins, he carefully corrected in his own
hand the errors in the Errata List.   Xerox copies of
the pages showing these handwritten corrections have
been added to this copy. "

Contains: "Orion, " "The Ruin, " "The Roots, " "Feast
Day, " "The Dancer, " "These Have the Future, " "The
Illusion, " "Seance, " "The Sides of a Mind, " "And from
Bad Dreams, " "December 31, 1939, " "The Masculine
Dead. "

Note: Everson signed the contract for the publication
of A3 in November 1941, and James Decker promised
to get the book out quickly.   After a series of delays,
The Masculine Dead was finally published, but was filled
with errors.   What follows is a letter (on file at the
Wm. Andrews Clark Library) written by Everson to
Decker upon the poet's receipt of his copies of A3:

                         Sept. 18, 1942
                         Rt. 1, Box 25
                         Selma, Calif.

Dear Decker:
            The books have arrived, and their ar-
rival brings home to me as has little else
ever done, what a complete fool I am.   For I
waited months beyond the time I could right-
fully expect publication, and did not protest,
nor hardly enquire, out of no other reason
than that you should not have to throw the book
together helter skelter, that it could never be
said that my impatience rendered imperfect
what would otherwise have been decently done.
From the tone of your letters I took you to be
a sincere trustworthy individual; I must have
been wrong; you crowded book after book in
ahead of mine, and then finally issued a volume
as hastily assembled as it would have been had
I wanted it last Christmas.
            For I believe I have the distinction of
placing my work on the market in about the
worst piece of composition I have ever seen in
a serious book of poems.   The typographical
errors are glaring enough (indeed, I do not
see how any compositor, in the most casual,
the most cursory survey of his work, overlooked some of those errors) but what really
appalls me is the violation done to certain of
my lines.   Why, in God's name, was I not
shown proofs?--if indeed any proofs were
pulled!   Is this ordinary, this essential co-
operative process between author and publisher too much to ask?   Was it again a question

of time? I'd have willingly waited another ten
months if such as this could have been avoided.
And why has it happened only to work of mine?
Every other volume of yours I've seen has
been scrupulously edited. It's been one of the
things I've admired you for.

But it is unthinkable that the book
should be released as it now stands. I have
no other recourse than to insist that you prepare the inclosed sheet of errata, that you
hold all the copies in your possession until you
have tabbed the sheets into them, that you send
me sufficient sheets to tab into the copies I
have here, that in the event you have already
sent copies for review, or have sold copies,
you immediately dispatch errata sheets to those
journals, booksellers, or persons. The injury
is beyond remedy; but nothing less will allevi-
ate a situation that is, by all standards, in-
tolerable.

Sincerely,

P.S.- I note that copyright is listed as being
held by the Press. Since I paid the fee, I
took it that copyright would belong to me.

Attached to the bottom of this typewritten letter is the
following handwritten note:

I wrote the above out of a deep sense of out-
rage and anger. Now, twenty four hours later,
fourteen of which were spent in the cannery
where I had time aplenty to think, I see that
outraged anger is too late. If I have been un-
just in anything I have said I apologize, but I
cannot see why it had to happen. I simply
cannot see why it had to happen. An hour with
my typescript, two more on the composing
stone, and all these defects would have gone--
save the crowding on pg. 13, which I could
have overlooked. How can you expect to sell
such work? I am almost too ashamed to show

it, much less take money for it; and I await
with apprehension the pronouncements of the
critics.

W. E.

A4   X WAR ELEGIES   1943

X WAR ELEGIES / [design] / by william everson /
[vertical:] illustrated by kemper nomland jr, untide
press, camp angel, waldport, oregon, 1943

[24 pp.].   22.8 x 15.4 cm.   Blue silk-screened wrappers: [in black, horizontal:] 10 / [in yellow, vertical:]
WAR / [in black, horizontal:] ELEGIES / [in yellow,
vertical:] WILLIAM EVERSON.   Brown paper, mimeographed.   Stapled and pasted.

Published by the Untide Press in 1943 in an edition of
1,000 copies at 10 cents.   Illustrations and typography
by Kemper Nomland, Jr.

Contains: A "Note" by the author, "X War Elegies,"
("The Vow," "Now in These Days," "One Born of This
Time," "The Unkillable Knowledge," "A Winter Ascent,"
"The Raid," "Weeds," "Night Scene," "To Sunder the
Rock").

Note: On an unknown number of copies, wrapper lettering is in black and red.   Text identical.   According to
William Everson, "After the original edition was ex-
hausted and orders kept coming in, other copies were
made from the original masters.   But when these wore
out, new ones were typed so variations crept in.   Total
number of copies mimeographed unknown."

A5   THE WALDPORT POEMS   1944

[in umber:] 1944 / W [in black:] ALDPORT POEMS /
William Everson / UNTIDE PRESS: WALDPORT, ORE-
GON   ILLUSTRATED BY CLAYTON JAMES

[32 pp.]. 24.3 x 16.5 cm. Decorative wrappers: [in black:] THE WALDPORT POEMS / [in umber: illustration] / [in black:] WILLIAM EVERSON. Linweave paper, Goudy light and Lydian types. Pages untrimmed, stapled.

Published in July, 1944, by the Untide Press in an edition of 975 copies at 25 cents. According to the colophon, the book was "executed upon a clam-action monster of incalculable vintage. It is the second printed publication of the Untide Press, the venture of a group of pacifists at Camp Angel, Waldport, Oregon, who, from under the mantle of conscription, submit it as one of the manifestations of those who seek to affirm the creative man."

Contains: A "Note" by the author; 11 untitled, numbered poems (later revised, became Part One of "Chronicle of Division").

A6   WAR ELEGIES   1944

WAR ELEGIES / [device] / William Everson / Illustrated by Kemper Nomland, Jr. / Untide Press, Waldport, Oregon / Nineteen Hundred Forty Four

[38 pp.]. 24.5 x 16.5 cm. Ochre wrappers. Decorative front cover: [in blue:] WAR ELEGIES / [in blue and black: illustration] / [in black:] William Everson. Pages untrimmed, stapled.

Published by the Untide Press in November, 1944, in an edition of 975 copies at 35 cents. Kemper Nomland's illustrations are in red and black. Some are included in A4; others are new to this edition.

Contains: "Note," "X War Elegies" (A4), with title of Elegy IV changed to ("London Address, February, 1941"); plus "Lay I in the Night," added as Elegy V.

Note: According to the colophon, "War Elegies is here presented in its first printed form. It was previously

issued by mimeograph in 1943 as the initial publication
of the Untide Press. The present printing contains in
addition War Elegy V, included here in its proper
chronological location. War Elegies is handset in
Goudy Light Oldstyle and Futura types. It has been
printed on Linweave Early American...."

A7   THE RESIDUAL YEARS   1944

[in red:] THE RESIDUAL YEARS / [illustration] / [in
black:] POEMS, 1940-1941 / WILLIAM EVERSON / THE
UNTIDE PRESS

[32 pp.].   22 x 18 cm.   Grey wrappers, mimeographed.
Illustrations on front cover and colophon page in red.
First lines in red, text in black.

Published by the Untide Press in an edition of 330 copies, December, 1944, at 15 cents. Designed by David
W. Jackson and William Eshelman, signed by the poet.

Contains: "Note" (by Everson). The poems are untitled
in this collection, their first lines serving as headings.
When the collection was reprinted in A9, the poems
were given their proper titles: "The Impossible
Choices," "The Presence," "The Approach," "Do You
Not Doubt," "Though Lying with Woman," "Lava Bed,"
"The Residual Years."

A8   POEMS: MCMXLII   1945

[in red:] poems: mcmxlii

[20 pp.].   24.4 x 16.3 cm.   Decorative printed wrappers: [in black: illustration] / [in red:] poems:
mcmxlii William Everson. Introductory poem, titles,
and colophon in red. Illustrations by Clayton James.
Stapled and pasted.

Printed by the poet in 1944-45 at the Untide Press,
Waldport, Oregon, in an edition of 500 copies at 20 cents.

Contains: "The Answer," "The City," "The Outlaw,"
"The Lovers," "Invocation," "The Growth," "The
Master," "The Citadel," "The Revolutionist," "The
Brothers," "The Friends," "The Divers," "The
Stranger," "The Divide" (and untitled prologue poem).

Note: Erratum slip follows "invocation." When published in A9, "The City" was titled "Hotel"; "The
Lovers," became "March"; "The Growth" was titled
"The Siege." In addition, the prologue poem became
the prologue to Part II of A9, and to Book One of A31.

A9 THE RESIDUAL YEARS   1948

[in black:] THE / RESIDUAL / YEARS / [in umber
and red: illustration] / [in black:] by WILLIAM EVER-
SON / [double rule] / A NEW DIRECTIONS BOOK

1 blank leaf, 148pp., 1 blank leaf. 23.3 x 16 cm.
Decorative paper covered boards in red and umber and
white, brown cloth-backed spine stamped in gold:
EVERSON / [device] / THE RESIDUAL YEARS. Set
in Weiss and Garamond types. Section numbers in red.
White endpapers. Issued in dust jacket.

Published in 1948 by New Directions in an edition of
1,000 copies, at $3.00. Printed by Peter Beilenson.

Contains: A5 ("The Waldport Poems"), "Chronicle of
Division," A4 ("X War Elegies"), A6 ("War Elegies"),
A7 ("The Residual Years"), A8 ("Poems: MCMXLII"),
selections made by Kenneth Rexroth from A1 ("These
Are the Ravens"), A2 ("San Joaquin"), A3 ("The Mascu-
line Dead"). All preceded by "Preface" (by Everson).

On September 19, 1936, William Everson wrote James
Laughlin at New Directions (in a letter on file at the
Wm. Andrews Clark Library) concerning The Residual
Years:

Dear James Laughlin,

    I should have replied to your letter of
August 18 long before now, but I could not
come to any terms within myself as to what I
should do. Since last writing I have moved up
here into the hill country south of Sebastapol,
which is itself some sixty miles north of San
Francisco, and am living with Hamilton and
Mary Tyler on their apple farm, setting about
organizing a permanent life here, putting up
the great Washington hand press I bought in
San Francisco, and making ready to launch
forth into the enterprise of writer-printer that
has so venerable a tradition in English Literature. It is a great dream, and I have nursed
it forward these many years now, through
those years in camp it always lay ahead of
me, and the formation of the old Untide Press
gave me to see how it could be done. Now I
stand close to it.

    But what held me off in writing to you
was the lack of certitude as to what I should
do about my past work. All my friends are
pressing for a comprehensive collection of
some kind, and the situation seems right now,
but exactly what [is] to be done I could not
know, and so hesitated to commit myself. Now
I have come to terms with the problem, have
arrived at a sense of proportion within myself
as to what I should do, and I submit it to you
to see whether or not it matches your own
ideas as to the kind of book of mine you would
care to bring out.

    It is a collection of my poetry written
over the last ten years, and includes a com-
bination of all the small editions I have published. It is called <u>The Residual Years:
Poems 1936-1946</u>, a title which is coming
more and more in my mind to stand as the
general title of my work as it progresses.
The format is arranged chronologically, year
by year, the years as sections, the sections
and the years amplifying the title, and giving

the book a wholeness of purpose, and a cumula-
tive extension no more casual a selection could
afford. It would terminate with the Chronicle
Of Division, of which I wrote earlier, which
embodies the last four years, and which is indeed the consummation of most of the elements
the earlier volumes traced, tentatively, seek-
ing for resolutions that had no answer, till the
great answer of the war made itself known,
unquestionably, and brought a great deal of material to a close.

I am aware that this close identification
of a body of poetry with the life of its writer
is now, at least among our severer critics,
not in favor. I remember all the objections
raised to your including photographs and holo-
graphs in your first Five Young American Poets. But I can conceive of no such divorce-
ment between my life and my work. I write
of my life and out of it. I draw constantly on
the incidents of it for material, and the ideas
within my poems refer back to the several
meanings of my life as it unfolds with the
teaching years. The years are the poems,
and the poems the years. It is the productive
impetus that brings out my best, and I cannot
relegate them to the incidental status of occasional pieces when in fact they are so inextri-
cably fused within the fabric of my life. It is
for these reasons that I am speaking for what
is essentially a collected edition rather than
the selected one you suggested. I cannot re-
move from among them pieces that were part
of their wholeness during creation. I have
favorites, of course, but each has its place,
each amplifies and reinforces the others. If
some err, they err in the element of excess,
never in insufficiency of motivation. There
may be a lurid bloom or two but there is no
dead wood. What was dead never got out of
the notebook. And published as development,
as growth, the lesser ones are sustained in
the forward-pushing context, are carried for-

ward from year to year; they take a logical
place they could never take as occasional
pieces.   As growth they are valid, and in
such a light I will stand by them all...

        With all good wishes--
                            William Everson

A10   A PRIVACY OF SPEECH   1949

[in black: illustration] / WILLIAM EVERSON / [in
red:] A PRIVACY OF SPEECH / [in black:] Ten poems
in sequence, with block print / decorations by Mary
Fabilli.   Printed at / The Equinox Press.   Berkeley,
California / 1949

5 blank leaves, 29 pp. , 1 leaf, 5 blank leaves.   26. 5 x
21 cm.   Grey decorative paper over boards, vellum
backed spine stamped in gold: A PRIVACY OF SPEECH.
Half-titles and section numbers in red.   Pages untrimmed.

Published by the Equinox Press in an edition of 100
copies in 1949, at $12. 50.   According to the colophon,
"This book, / which is the first book of The Equinox
Press, / was made by William Everson: / designed,
handset and printed on the handpress. / The types used
are Centaur & Arrighi. / The paper is Tovil, an English handmade, printed damp. / Done in an edition of
100 copies, / it has been completed on Candlemas Day,
1949, / and becomes a step toward that visionary book
of the imagination, / which is the printer's hope, /
and to which he is once more committed. "

Contains: "A Privacy of Speech. "

Note: Received "highest Honors" in the Rounce & Coffin
Club "Western Books" selection.

A11   TRIPTYCH FOR THE LIVING   1951

[in black: illustration] / [in red: device] / [in black:]
triptych for the living / poems by william everson,
with prints / by mary fabilli.   the seraphim press:
1951

3 blank leaves, 26 pp., 2 leaves, 3 blank leaves.
26. 8 x 21. 2 cm.   Bound in goat vellum, with orange
cloth ties.   Hammer Uncial type on Tovil paper.
Pages untrimmed.

Published by the Seraphim Press in 1951 in an edition
of 200 copies, of which fewer than 100 were issued (remaining sheets destroyed), at $12. 50.   Printed and
bound by William Everson.

Contains: "Triptych for the Living" ("The Uncouth, "
"The Coming, " "The Wise"), "Making of the Cross, "
"Flight in the Desert, " "The Massacre of the Holy
Innocents. "

Colophon: "... The book in its design looks back toward the primitive church in search of a model appro-
priate to the apostolic character of the text.   For
though the church triumphant exists as such only in
heaven, its spirit was certainly anticipated in the massive & resplendant volumes of medieval christendom,
from which our subsequent convention of religious typography developed.   But the church militant evolved
its own book-forms many centuries earlier, and these
Latin codexes, with their comparative lightness, and
the open quality of their pages, are nearer to our
present tastes; so that the current revival of the uncial,
as well as the tragic similarity of the times, provide
sufficient occasion to warrant this backward glance.
Books as we know them (sheets folded together &
sewn) were born in the catacombs, where an incorrigi-
ble age was purged of its excesses; and where our age,
if we heed not, will be purged in the anguish of its
own. "

A12   AT THE EDGE   1952

At The Edge

Broadside.   52. 2 x 40 cm.

100 copies of this broadside were printed by Brother
Antoninus in 1952.   Goudy Newstyle type on Kelmscott
Hammer & Anvil paper.   Of the about 80 copies remaining in 1958, all were offered for sale by the Albertus Magnus Press framed and signed by the poet at
$ 7. 50.   There were two types of frames, one black,
the other light brown.   Frame: 53 x 46. 5 cm.

For the 1958 release, the poet wrote a prospectus describing the origin, significance, and printing of the
poem.   In addition to being used as a means of announcing the poem, a copy of the prospectus was attached to the back of each copy of the poem framed in
black.   The greater part of the edition was framed in Berkeley by a professional framer (in black), one at a time,
as the orders came in.   The remaining copies were
taken by a gallery in Los Angeles and were all framed
at once (in brown).

A13   TRIPTYCH FOR THE LIVING   1955

[verso of front cover] TRIPTYCH FOR THE LIVING
[device] By BROTHER ANTONINUS [device] O. P. /
[device] The Uncouth [device] The Coming [device] The
Wise

[12 pp.].   13 x 20 cm.   Cream printed wrappers:
[recto of front cover:]   BROTHER ANTONINUS [device]
O. P. / triptych / ALBERTUS MAGNUS PRESS.   Decorative initials.   American Uncial type on Tovil paper.
Sewn, pages untrimmed.

According to the colophon, this item was to be printed
in an edition of 200 copies by William Everson on the
Albertus Magnus Press in 1955.   All of the sheets were
printed, but only two copies were cut and sewn into cov-

ers.   Everson retains one, another was given to a
friend.   Never released due to error on p. 10, ℓ. 5:
"up" has been omitted following "can get."

Contains: "Triptych for the Living."

A14   A FRAGMENT FOR THE BIRTH OF GOD   1958

[in black:] a [in terra-cotta:] F [in black:] ragment for
the birth of God

1 p.   12.7 x 19.8 cm.   The poem is printed on one
leaf of uniform size and laid in folded sheet.   Title
on front cover.   Issued in cream colored envelope of
same paper stock.

Published by the Albertus Magnus Press, May, 1958, in
an edition of 1,000 copies (of which about 800 were destroyed in 1959).   Available as a souvenir of the poet's
reading at the St. Thomas Aquinas Institute in May,
1958.

Contains: "A Fragment for the Birth of God."

Note: In 1959 this poem was printed by Everson in an
edition of 6,000 copies as the St. Albert's College
Christmas card.   Title in terra-cotta, a woodblock
print by Everson of Madonna and Child on front cover.
French fold.   10.8 x 22.2 cm.   Issued in envelope as
above.   Again issued in 1963.

A15   AN AGE INSURGENT   1959

[printed wrappers:] AN AGE INSURGENT / Poems by
Brother Antoninus, O.P. / Blackfriars Publications /
Blackfriars of the West / San Francisco / twenty-five
cents

[20 pp.].   17 x 12.3 cm.   Black printed wrappers.
Stapled.

Published by Blackfriars Publications in May, 1959, in
an edition of 500 copies, at 25 cents. According to
Everson, probably fewer than 100 were issued. There
are a large number of errors in the text.

Contains: Author's Note, "In the Dream's Recess,"
"Triptych for the Living," "The Making of the Cross,"
"The Flight in the Desert," "The Quittance," "Past
Solstice," "Advent," "Canticle to the Waterbirds," "The
Encounter," "Out of the Ash."

A16 a. THE CROOKED LINES OF GOD   1959

[in black:] the / crooked lines / of God / [in red:]
Poems 1949-1954 / [in black:] By Brother Antoninus /
Contemporary Poets Series / The University of Detroit
Press [device] 1959

88p., 1 leaf, 1 blank leaf.   21.5 x 22.2 cm.   Gray
paper covered boards: [front and back:] [in red: fancy
rule] / [in black:] the crooked lines of God / [in red:
fancy rule].   Black cloth-backed spine, stamped in gold:
Brother Antoninus / [device] / the crooked lines of
God. Centaur and American Uncial types, Utopian paper. Decorative initials. White endpapers. Issued
with dust jacket.

Published in 1959 by the University of Detroit Press in
an edition of 1,000 copies, at $4.00.   Number one in
the Detroit Contemporary Poets Series. Printed by
William Everson at the Albertus Magnus Press, St. Albert's College, Oakland, California.

Contains: "Foreword: These Crooked Lines,"
"Triptych," "The Flight in the Desert," "The Making
of the Cross," "Gethsemani," "The Screed of the
Flesh," "The Massacre of the Holy Innocents," "A
Canticle to the Waterbirds," "The Encounter," "A
Penitential Psalm," "Hospice of the Word," "A Jubilee
for St. Peter Martyr," "A Savagery of Love," "The
Month of the Dead," "A Canticle to the Christ in the
Holy Eucharist," "The South Coast," "Annul in Me My
Manhood," "Out of the Ash."

Note: An unknown number of copies have a sheet
folded incorrectly so that pp. 49-50 and pp. 59-60 are
out of sequence.

A16 b. Second edition issued April, 1960, in an edition of 1,000 copies. Identical with A16a, with these
changes: copyright pages designate "Second Edition,"
colophon device is in red, colophon date is April, 1960.
Printed by William Everson, with several corrections
and additions in the text. Issued in dust jacket.

A16 c. Third edition of 1,000 copies produced by photo
lithography and released in 1962. 500 copies bound in
black cloth over boards. Cover designs omitted, spine
stamp identical to A16a. Issued in dust jacket. 500
copies in paper wrappers, binding identical to dust
jacket.

Note: Second impression of third edition of 500 copies
issued in 1964, cloth bound as A16c.

A17   THERE WILL BE HARVEST   1960

[in black:] There Will Be Harvest / [in rust:] William
Everson / [in black: illustration]

[2 pp.]. 26.3 x 19.8 cm. Title and illustration in
rust, text in black. French fold, pages untrimmed.

Printed by Kenneth J. Carpenter in an edition of 200
copies for the joint meeting of the Zamorano and Rox-
burghe Clubs, September, 1960, in Berkeley, California.

According to the colophon, "This poem, There Will Be
Harvest, is part of an unpublished sequence by the
same name written in the fall of 1947, some four years
before the author became Brother Antoninus of the Dominican Order. At the time Everson was employed at
the University of California Press, and the printing reference commemorates the moving of his giant Washington handpress from the Tyler ranch on the ridge west

of Sebastopol to the Maybeck House on Ashby Avenue
in Berkeley, where The Equinox Press was formally
founded.   This is the only reference to printing in the
poet-printer's verse. "

Contains: "There Will Be Harvest. "

A18   THE YEAR'S DECLENSION   1961

[in black:] The / [in red:] Y [in black:] ear's / [in
red:] D [in black:] eclension / by William Everson /
Berkeley: 1961

[36 pp.].   29. 2 x 21 cm.   Grey paper over boards with
design (in red and black) on front.   Title and contents
pages printed in red and black.   Titles and decorations
in red, text in black.   Initials are oversized.   Woodcuts
by Kenneth John Carpenter.

Published in 1961 in an edition of 100 unnumbered copies signed by the poet.   Printed by Kenneth John Carpenter on the Berkeley Albion in the Rare Books Department of the General Library of the University of
California at Berkeley.

Contains: "Rainy Easter, " "Two Lives, " "Under a
Keeping Spring, " "The First Absence, I, " "The First
Absence, II, " "The Quarrel, " "Court of Law, " "The
Dance, " "The Dusk, " "End of Summer, " "In the Dream's
Recess, " "Dead Winter. "

Note: Written in 1948 in Berkeley, California.

A19   THE HAZARDS OF HOLINESS   1962

THE HAZARDS / OF HOLINESS / POEMS 1957-1960 /
by Brother Antoninus / DOUBLEDAY & COMPANY,
INC. / GARDEN CITY, NEW YORK, 1962

94pp. , 1 blank leaf.   21. 5 x 14. 7 cm.   Red cloth over
boards, gold stamped: [front cover] THE HAZARDS /

OF HOLINESS; [spine:] THE HAZARDS OF HOLINESS /
Brother Antoninus / DOUBLEDAY.   White endpapers.
Issued in dust jacket.

Published by Doubleday in 1962 in an edition of 2,000
copies, at $2.25.   A second printing of 1,000 copies,
and a third printing of 2,000 copies were issued with
no changes in text or binding, at $3.50.

Contains: "Foreword," "Jacob and the Angel," "All the
Way to Heaven," "A Siege of Silence," "Passion Week,"
"Zone of Death," "What Birds Were There," "Saints,"
"You, God," "A Frost Lay White on California," "I Am
Long Weaned," "In the Breach," "Sleep-tossed I Lie,"
"The Word," "Black Christ," "A Canticle to the Great
Mother of God," "In All These Acts," "God Germed in
Raw Granite," "The Song the Body Dreamed," "The
Hazards of Holiness," "The Conversion of Saint Paul,"
"In Savage Wastes."

A20   THE POET IS DEAD   1964

[in black:] A Memorial for Robinson Jeffers / by
Brother Antoninus / [in purple:] The Poet Is Dead /
[in black:] The Auerhahn Press / San Francisco:
mcmlxiv

[28 pp.].   26.7 x 20.7 cm.   Cream paper over boards,
spine backed with 1/4 oasis leather.   White paper
pasted on spine, in gold: THE POET IS DEAD.   Pages
untrimmed.

Published in an edition of 205 signed copies, of which
5 are boxed in cream fabric boards and not for sale,
by Auerhahn Press, March, 1964, at $12.50.   Dedi-
cated to Lawrence Clark Powell.

Contains: "A Note," "The Poet Is Dead."

Note: "To be read with a full stop between the
strophes, as in a dirge."   Device between strophes in
purple.

A21   THE ROSE OF SOLITUDE   1964

The Rose of Solitude

Broadside.   43.7 x 30.3 cm.   Edges untrimmed.

Published by Oyez as "Oyez Number Two" in 1964 in an
edition of 350 copies, at $1.50.   Printed by the Auer-
hahn Press, San Francisco.   In 1965, a series of ten
broadsides, including A21, were placed together in a
linen covered board folder with a black cloth tie, 45.7
x 33 cm.   Printed white paper pasted on cover: [in
umber:] POEMS IN BROADSIDE / [in black:] Michael
McClure: Brother Antoninus / Josephine Miles: Robert Duncan: Robert Creeley / [in umber:] OYEZ / [in
black:] David Meltzer: Denise Levertov: Charles Ol-
son / Gary Snyder: William Bronk / [in umber:]
FIRST SERIES.   Twenty-five copies of this set were offered for sale.

Contains: "The Rose of Solitude."

A22   THE BLOWING OF THE SEED   1966

[in black:] William Everson / [in gold:] THE BLOWING
OF THE SEED / [in black:] Henry W. Wenning / New
Haven / mcmlxvi

[32 pp.].   26.8 x 16.5 cm.   Decorative red, brown,
and cream paper over boards [imitation marble]; leather
spine, blind stamped: [reversed] [line] / Everson /
[device] / The Blowing of the Seed / [line].   End papers, edges untrimmed.

Published in 1966 by Henry W. Wenning in an edition
of 218 copies, at $17.50.   According to the colophon,
"of ccxviii copies, all on Kochi and signed by the poet,
copies xv to ccxv are for sale.   The first three copies
lettered a, b, and c are, respectively, for poet, publisher, and printer.   Copies i-xv are for friends of the
poet and publisher."   Printed by Claude Fredericks.
Signed by the poet on page prior to colophon, which appears prior to title page.

Contains: Untitled introductory poem, "Prologue," six untitled numbered poems, "Epilogue." (The introductory poem, later titled "The Sphinx," was collected as the prologue to Book Three of A31.)

Note: Also according to colophon, "This sequence was written in mcmxlvi and belongs to the period of The Residual Years. For several reasons it was not included in that book and is here and now published for the first time."

A23   SINGLE SOURCE   1966

[in umber] SINGLE SOURCE / [in black:] The Early Poems of William Everson / [1934-1940] / Introduction by Robert Duncan / OYEZ [device] BERKELEY

ix-xiii, 105 pp., 1 leaf, 1 blank leaf.   24 x 15.7 cm. Light brown paper over boards, cover illustration in black.   Chocolate brown linen-backed spine, gold stamped: SINGLE SOURCE / William Everson / OYEZ. Section Titles in umber.   White endpapers.   Issued in dust jacket, with notes by Everson.

Published by Oyez in 1966, at $4.50, in an edition of 1,000 copies, of which 25 were bound by hand by Dorothy Hawley and numbered and signed by the poet, at $12.00. Designed and printed by Graham Mackintosh.

Contains: "Introduction by Robert Duncan," A1 ("These Are the Ravens"), A2 ("San Joaquin"), A3 ("The Masculine Dead").   Corrects A3 and adds a new ending.

Note: Unknown number of copies spell language langauge, p. ix, ℓ. 16-17.

A24   THE ROSE OF SOLITUDE /
       ROSA DE SOLEDAD   1966

[in umber:] The Rose of Solitude / Rosa de Soledad

Folded broadside. 38 x 25 cm. Printed cover: [in umber:] OYEZ. Edges untrimmed.

Published by Oyez in 1966. Printed by Graham Mackintosh, the broadside was issued as a Christmas poem from the publisher.

Contains: "The Rose of Solitude," "Rosa de Soledad."

Note: English and Spanish texts of the poem face each other. Spanish translation done by Catherine de Rodriguez.

A25   THE VISION OF FELICITY   1966

The Vision of Felicity

Broadside. 38.2 x 25.5 cm. Block print by Karyl Klopp.

Printed on hand-press by the Lowell House Printers, April, 1966, in an edition of 65 signed copies. Written by Brother Antoninus in New York City, 1963.

A26   THE ROSE OF SOLITUDE   1967

THE ROSE / OF SOLITUDE / by Brother Antoninus / Doubleday & Company, Inc. / 1967 [device] Garden City, New York

xiv pp., 1 leaf, 125 pp., 1 blank leaf.   21.5 x 14.5. Burgundy cloth covered boards with black cloth spine, gold stamped: Brother Antoninus / THE ROSE OF SOLITUDE / Doubleday. Burgundy end papers. Issued in dust jacket.

Published by Doubleday in an edition of 5,000 copies, May, 1967, at $3.95. The Commonwealth Club of California awarded the poet the Silver Medal for the best book of poetry published by a California poet in 1967.

Contains: "Foreword," "Prologue," "Part One, I Nail
My Life": "The Way of Life and the Way of Death,"
"The Kiss of the Cross," "Immortal Strangeness"; "Part
Two, Fire in Ice": "The Canticle of the Rose," "The
Rose of Solitude," "The Afterglow of the Rose"; "Part
Three, Deliver Me Whole": "On the Thorn," "The Un-
derlying Torsion," "The Vision of Felicity," "I Eat Life
Back"; "Part Four, What Freedom Is": "From the Rock
Untombed," "The Raging of the Rose"; "Part Five, I
Originate Death": "The Face I Know."

Note: Subtitle, "A Love Poem-Sequence," appears only
on dust jacket.

A27   IN THE FICTIVE WISH   1967

[in red:] IN THE / FICTIVE / WISH / [in black:]
William Everson / [in red:] OYEZ

7-22 pp., 1 leaf. 30.5 x 21.7 cm. Maroon covered
boards. Spine stamped: [in gold: 2 rules] / [black
background, stamped in gold:] IN THE FICTIVE WISH /
[in gold: 2 rules]. Orange endpapers, pages untrimmed. Illustration in black, first half-title in black,
second half-title and section numbers in red.

Published in 1967 by Oyez in an edition of 200 copies
signed by the author, at $20.00. Woodcut by Mary
Fabilli. According to the colophon, "This book has
been designed and printed from hand-set Centaur and
Arrighi type on handmade Fabriano by Graham Mackintosh, and bound by the Schuberth Book Bindery."

Contains: "In the Fictive Wish."

Notes: "In the Fictive Wish" was written in Cascade
Locks, Oregon, spring, 1946; the last of the four poems
was written in Berkeley, 1947. Prospectus written by
Everson. An unauthorized edition of A27 exists. It is
bound in blue wrappers, printed in offset. Contains a
few corrections in ballpoint. Number of copies and date
unknown.

A28   A CANTICLE TO THE WATERBIRDS   1968

Brother Antoninus / A CANTICLE TO THE WATER-
BIRDS / Photographs By Allen Say / EIZO / Berkeley
/ 1968

[40 pp.]. 17 plates. 22.2 x 19.8 cm. Grey boards,
stamped in black on front cover: A Canticle To The
Waterbirds. End papers.

Published in 1968 by EIZO, Berkeley, in an edition of
200 copies, at $30.00. Numbered and signed by both
the poet and the photographer. Printed by Lawton and
Alfred Kennedy of San Francisco.

Contains: "Writing the Waterbirds," and "A Canticle to
the Waterbirds."

Note: An edition of 2,000 copies bound in paper was
issued simultaneously, at $3.00. Cover photographs.
Spine: A Canticle To The Waterbirds / Eizo Press.
Identical to A28.

A29   ROBINSON JEFFERS:
       FRAGMENTS OF AN OLDER FURY   1968

[in red:] Robinson Jeffers: / Fragments of an Older
Fury / [in black:] By Brother Antoninus / Oyez: 1968

xv pp., 173 pp., 5 leaves. 23.5 x 16 cm. Light
brown cloth covered boards, gold stamped spine:
Robinson Jeffers: Fragments of an Older Fury [device]
Brother Antoninus [device] Oyez. Chapter titles in
red, decorative initials in black.

Published by Oyez in 1968 in a trade edition at $7.50.

Contains: "Foreword," "Not Without Wisdom," "The
Giant Hand," "Post Mortem," "The Beauty of God,"
"Hellenistics," "The Far-Cast Spear," "The Poet Is
Dead," "List of Works Cited," "Index of Names."

A30   THE SPRINGING OF THE BLADE   1968

[in black:] The [in green: design] [in black:] Springing /
of the Blade

half-title: Poems of / Nineteen forty seven / by
William Everson

half-title: Printed in / Nineteen sixty eight / The
Black Rock Press

[48 pp.]. 33 x 25.1 cm. Green covered boards, light
green design stamped on front cover. Spine stamped in
light green: THE SPRINGING OF THE BLADE. Green
endpapers, pages untrimmed.

Published by the Black Rock Press in 1968 in an edition
of 180 copies. Colophon: "Printed on an 1837 super-
royal Columbian handpress by Kenneth J. Carpenter,
The Black Rock Press, Reno, Nevada. Presswork began March, 1966, and was completed November, 1967.
The type is sixteen point Bembo, hand set; the paper
is Rives, printed damp. 180 copies / The printing of
this book was made possible only with the encourage-
ment and assistance of the Desert Research Institute's
Committee on Research Planning for the Humanities of
the University of Nevada, David Magee and Patricia H.
Carpenter. / Some of these poems previously appeared
in The Pacific Spectator and Tiger's Eye. / Once again
it has been a privilege to print the work of a fine poet,
a treasured friend. / K.J.C."

Contains: "The Iron Dimension," "Odor of Autumn,"
"Yellow Weather," "Muscat," "Carrousel," "Areas of
Corruption," "There Will Be Harvest" (six untitled
poems).

Note: The poet's signature appears on p. 1.

A31   THE RESIDUAL YEARS   1968

William Everson / THE RESIDUAL / YEARS / Poems

Brother Antoninus / William Everson

THE RESIDUAL YEARS

Poems 1934-1948

All the verse of the celebrated San Francisco poet written before his crisis of religious faith

William Everson   THE RESIDUAL YEARS   NDP263

THE RESIDUAL YEARS

Poems 1934–1948

Photograph by Allen Say

Brother Antoninus / William Everson

Introduction by Kenneth Rexroth

When New Directions first published *The Residual Years* in 1948, its author, William Everson, was a young man working in California. Not long before, he had been released from a work camp for conscientious objectors, where, with a few other writers and a mimeograph machine, he had set up the Untide Press which published some of the most influential protest poetry of World War II.

Today, nearly twenty years after his conversion to Catholicism, William Everson is the Dominican monk Brother Antoninus, known for his readings across the country and one of the most celebrated figures in the current revival of Catholic poetry.

The Residual Years is a landmark of a period in our history, the aftermath of the Depression and the turmoil of the War. But more than that, it is a candid, revealing record of a poet's, and a man's, spiritual growth. Antoninus has written recently of the book that "its roots go back to the earth of the San Joaquin Valley, the substratum of my life, back to a happy marriage, inexorable incarceration in the Waldport Camp, painful divorce, hopeful remarriage, and abrupt, disturbing separation—back to my love of nature and of woman, to a poetry of physical celebration and tortured sensuality; back, in a word, to 'the residual years,' a reservoir of experience which still holds the deep energies of response and sustenance that feed my religious spirit."

A New Directions Book   NDP263 $2.25

1934-1948 / The Pre-Catholic Poetry of Brother Antoninus / With an Introduction by Kenneth Rexroth / A
New Directions Book

xvii pp., 238 pp.   20.8 x 14 cm.   Red cloth covered
boards, spine stamped in black: William Everson /
THE RESIDUAL YEARS / New Directions.   White endpapers.   Issued in dust jacket.

Published in October, 1968, by New Directions in an
edition of 3,000 copies, at $6.50.

Contains: Introduction by Kenneth Rexroth, A1, A2, A3,
A4, A5, A6, A7, A10, A18, A22, A27, A30, Index.

Note: A paper edition of 3,000 copies was issued simultaneously, at $2.25.   Identical to A31; pictorial
wrapper identical to dust jacket.   Has gone through a
second printing.

A32   THE CITY DOES NOT DIE   1969

THE CITY / DOES NOT DIE / [rule] / BROTHER /
ANTONINUS / [rule] / DEDICATED TO / JOSEPH
ALIOTO, MAYOR / OF SAN FRANCISCO / AND READ
OUT BY THE / AUTHOR AT THE / CEREMONIES /
COMMEMORATING THE / SAN FRANCISCO / EARTH-
QUAKE / April 18 / 1969

8 pp.   23.9 x 15.8 cm.   Light blue, printed wrappers.
On verso of front cover: At the Dawn of the Aquarian
Age / [device] / Copyright 1969 By Brother Antoninus.

Published by Oyez in 1969 in an edition of 2,000 copies.

Contains: "The City Does Not Die."

A33   THE LAST CRUSADE   1969

[in black:] THE LAST / CRUSADE / [in red: heraldic
device] / [in black:] BROTHER ANTONINUS / [in red:]
OYEZ

3 leaves, 23 pp., 1 leaf, 1 blank leaf, 1 leaf.   33 x
24.2 cm.   Cream fabric covered boards, vellum spine
stamped in gold: The Last Crusade / [device] / Brother
Antoninus.   First half-title in red and black; second and
third half-titles, initials, and page numbers in red.
Set in Van Dijck, printed on Arches.   White endpapers,
pages untrimmed.   Clear plastic dust jacket.

Published by Oyez in 1969 in an edition of 165 copies
numbered and signed by the poet, at $35.00.   Designed
and printed by Graham Mackintosh, bound by Jack Grey.

Contains: "The Last Crusade," "A Note to the Last
Crusade."

Note: While the colophon specified 165 copies, the
bindery delivered 180 copies to the publisher.   165 of
these were numbered and signed by the poet; the remainder went out for review (unsigned and un-numbered).
Prospectus for the volume was written by Everson.
"The Last Crusade" was written in 1958.

A34   EARTH POETRY   1971

[in black:] William Everson / [in umber:] earth poetry

[4 pp.].   50.8 x 32.8 cm.   Folio pamphlet, with a
cover leaf, interior sheet folded for 4 pp. of text,
double columned.   Cover leaf features a photograph of
the poet by Allen Say.

Published by Oyez in July, 1971, at $3.50.   Designed
and printed by Graham Mackintosh.

Contains: "Earth Poetry."

Note: Erratum, p. (2), col. 2, ℓ. 22, "myself" should
read "mystery."

A35   ARCHETYPE WEST   1971

ARCHETYPE WEST / The Pacific Coast As A Literary

Region / by / William Everson / Commissioned by /
American Libraries / Chicago / Written at Stinson
Beach, California / Feb. to Feb. / 1970 - 71

1 leaf, 106 pp. 21.5 x 28 cm. Black plastic spiral
binding.

Typed and xeroxed by the poet in an edition of 10 presentation copies. This is the first edition of an essay
later expanded and corrected in E43 and A41. Contains
corrections by the author in red ink and pencil.

Contains: "Archetype West."

A36   WHO IS SHE THAT LOOKETH FORTH
         AS THE MORNING   1972

[Illustration in yellow, green, blue] / [in black:] WHO
IS SHE THAT LOOKETH / FORTH AS THE MORNING /
Brother Antoninus / Capricorn Press 1972 Santa Bar-
bara

1 blank leaf, 2 leaves, 1-19 pp., 1 blank leaf, 2
leaves. 32.2 x 26.3 cm. Green fabricord stamped in
gold on front [illustration] and spine: WHO IS SHE
THAT LOOKETH FORTH AS THE MORNING / [device]
/ Brother Antoninus. Endpapers are printed from
acrylic patterns using water-based inks. (Note: On
two examined copies, colors vary considerably from
dark blue to light green.) Title page blocks cut by
Graham Mackintosh. Printed on Curtis Rag from
Trump Mediaeval type and hand bound by Earle Grey.
Clear plastic dust jacket. Text in black; Initial, page
numbers, and epigram in blue.

Published in 1972 by Capricorn Press in an edition of
250 copies numbered and signed by the poet. Designed
and printed by Noel Young.

Contains: "Who Is She That Looketh Forth As the
Morning," "A Note" (by the poet).

Notes: Another copy examined (248), pp. 3-(10) are
trimmed 1.3 and .6 cm. shorter than the rest. A
paperback edition of A35 was issued with text identical
to limited edition. Publisher places number of copies
at 1500, although the poet recalls the edition size as
500 copies. Written in 1963.

A37   GALE AT DAWN   1972

Gale at Dawn / by William Everson

Broadside.   52 x 39.8 cm.   Tovil handmade paper,
Goudy Oldstyle type, printed on an 1830 Acorn Handpress.   Decorative initial hand-done in blue.   Pages
untrimmed.

Published by the Lime Kiln Press in an edition of 200
copies signed by the poet in 1972, at $35.00 for set.
Included in portfolio "West to the Water," printed as a
Handpress Workshop project by Malcolm Blanchard,
Todd Hirozawa, Rik Isensee, and Tom Whitridge under
the direction of William Everson.   Also includes poems
by George Hitchcock, Mary Norbert Korte, Peter Veb-
len, Naomi Clark, and John Skinner.

Contains: "Gale at Dawn."

Notes: Prospectus lists Everson's poem as "Landwind at
Dawn."   The calligraphy was done by various hands.
Sets 26-50 were penned by Everson.   A further set, 76-
100, was also done by Everson, but under the pseudonym
of Phillip Dorn.   Prospectus written by Everson.

A38   TENDRIL IN THE MESH   1973

[in black:] William Everson / [in gold:] Tendril / in the
[in rust:] Mesh / [in black:] Cayucos Books 1973

[44 pp.].   31.1 x 21.3 cm.   Decorated paper covered
boards, 1/8 vellum covered spine blind stamped: TEN-
DRIL IN THE MESH.   Titles in rust and gold; section
numbers in rust.   Pages untrimmed.

Published by Cayucos Books in 1973 in an edition of
250 numbered copies signed by the poet, at $37.50.
Designed and printed by Clifford Burke at Cranium
Press, San Francisco, bound by the Cardoza-James
Bindery, San Francisco. Prospectus written by Ever-
son.

Contains: "Tendril in the Mesh."

Note: Advertisement announces 50 pp.

A39   BLACK HILLS   1973

BLACK HILLS / [device] WILLIAM EVERSON /
DIDYMUS PRESS

[20 pp.].   30.3 x 25 cm.   Boards covered in handmade
grey rice papers, light brown linen-backed spine stamped
in gold: BLACK HILLS / DIDYMUS PRESS. White endpapers, pages untrimmed.

Published by Didymus Press in August, 1973, in an edition of 285 copies, of which 200 were for sale, at
$12.50.   Illustrated by Thayer Hopkins, printed by
Thomas Whitridge.   Numbered and signed by the
poet.

Contains: "Black Hills."

Note: Prospectus contains "Apologia" by Everson regarding the writing of "Black Hills."

A40   MAN-FATE   1974

William Everson / MAN-FATE / The Swan Song of
Brother Antoninus / A New Directions Book

[ix pp.], 80 pp., 3 blank leaves.   20.8 x 14 cm.
Green cloth covered boards, spine stamped in black:
WILLIAM EVERSON / MAN-FATE / NEW DIRECTIONS.
White endpapers.   Issued in dust jacket.

MAN-FATE

The Swan Song of Brother Antoninus

WILLIAM EVERSON

"These are the poems of a man undergoing a major break fairly late in his years," explains William Everson in his preface to *Man-Fate*. It is his first collection since leaving the Dominican order in December 1969, and with it the name of Brother Antoninus, by which he was known for twenty years as one of the foremost Catholic poets of our time. The book, he continues, "is a love poem sequence, a cycle of renewal, but it also concerns the monastic life, from the point of view of one who has renounced it. The love of woman and the love of solitude have contested together, and solitude has lost."

"Tendril in the Mesh," the longest poem in *Man-Fate*, was written while the author was still living the life of a Dominican brother. Because it is the last piece in which he speaks in the persona of a monk, it gives to the entire collection its definitive subtitle: *The Swan Song of Brother Antoninus*. After the first public reading of "Tendril," Everson tells us, he "stripped off his religious habit and fled the platform." The fifteen other poems in the book complete the cycle of reversion from religious to secular life.

[Also by William Everson: *The Residual Years: Poems 1934–1948*, $6.50 & New Directions Paperback 263, $2.25]

*Cover drawing by Salim Patell; photograph by John Arms;
design by Gertrude Huston*

A NEW DIRECTIONS PAPERBOOK   NDP369 $2.75

WILLIAM EVERSON   MAN-FATE   NDP369

Published by New Directions in 1974 at $6.95.

Contains: "Preface," A38 ("Tendril in the Mesh"),
A37 ("Gale at Dawn"), A39 ("Black Hills"), "Ebb at
Evening," "The Man-Fate," "Seed," "The Gauge,"
"Socket of Consequence," "The Gash," "'A Time to
Mourn,'" "Storm at Low Tide," "The Narrows of
Birth," "The Challenge," "The Scout," "The Dunes,"
"Dark Waters," "Note," Index.

Note: A paper edition was issued simultaneously at
$2.75. Identical to A40.

A41   ARCHETYPE WEST   1976

[thin rule border] / ARCHETYPE WEST: / THE
PACIFIC COAST AS / A LITERARY REGION / [rule] /
William Everson / OYEZ / Berkeley 1976

xiv pp., 181 pp. 23.6 x 15.8 cm. Black cloth covered boards, gold stamped front cover: William Everson / ARCHETYPE WEST: / THE PACIFIC COAST /
AS A LITERARY REGION. Gold stamped spine: William Everson / ARCHETYPE WEST / OYEZ. White
endpapers. Issued in dust jacket.

Published in 1976 by Oyez in a trade edition at $8.95.
Jacket photograph by Dave Bohn.

Contains: "Acknowledgements," "Foreword," "Preface,"
"Archetype West," "Notes," "Appendix: Inception of the
Archetype," "Notes to the Appendix," "Index."

Note: A paper edition at $3.95 was issued simultaneous-
ly by Oyez. Text identical with A41.

A42   RIVER-ROOT   1976

[in black:] William Everson / [in rust: illustration] /
[in black:] River-Root / A Syzygy for the Bicentennial
of These States / Oyez 1976

2 blank leaves, 50, [1] pp., 1 leaf, 1 blank leaf. 32
x 25 cm. Light grey boards with illustration on front
and back in rust. Leather spine stamped in gold:
William Everson / River-Root [device] A Syzygy /
Oyez. Rust endpapers, pages untrimmed.

Published by Oyez in 1976 in an edition of 250 copies,
of which 200 were for sale, signed by the poet, at
$50.00. Illustrations by Patrick Kennedy. Designed
by Thomas Whitridge, bound by Cardoza-James.

Dedication: "In preparing this manuscript for publication, its / specifically American character became
more keenly / impressed upon me than I had earlier
felt it. And I / realized that in issuing it during this
200th anniversary / of our founding I am, in effect, of-
fering it as a poet's / gift to the Nation; and so dedi-
cate it, as Whitman / might have, to the Bicentennial
of these States."

Contains: "River-Root," "Author's Afterword."

Note: A softcover trade edition of A42 was published
by Oyez in 1976 in an edition of 5,000 copies at $2.95.
Illustrations in black. The afterword was replaced with
a new "Introduction" by the poet. Some corrections in
the text.

A43   MISSA DEFUNCTORUM   1976

Broadside. 59 x 44 cm. Hammer & Anvil paper,
edges untrimmed; Weiss type. Untitled, with woodcut
by William Everson. Decorative initial in red.

Fifty-four copies of this broadside were printed by the
poet at the Lime Kiln Press. All are signed in pencil
and numbered. Completed in November, 1976, these
broadsides were not for sale.

Contains: "Missa Defunctorum."

B. BOOKS WITH INTRODUCTIONS BY WILLIAM EVERSON

B1   NOVUM PSALTERIUM PII XII   1955

[in umber:] NOVUM / PSALTERIUM / PII XII / [in black:] AN UNFINISHED FOLIO / EDITION OF BROTHER ANTONINUS, O. P. / LOS ANGELES / MCMLV

xxviii pp. , 6 leaves, 1-88pp. , 17-76 pp. , 1 leaf, 1 blank leaf. 39. 9 x 26. 5 cm. Blue Morocco leather boards, tooled spine gold stamped: [cover:] [decorative cross] / NOVUM PSALTERIUM / PII XII; [spine:] [four rules] / NOVUM / PSALTER- / IUM / PII XII / [four rules] / [four rules] / [four rules] / [four rules]. Inside covers: double gold rule around margins: bottom front cover verso: THE LAKESIDE PRESS, CHICAGO. Titles in umber, text in black. White end-papers, pages untrimmed.

Note: Verso of second leaf contains: COPY NUMBER / [16] / PRESENTED BY / COUNTESS ESTELLE DOHENY / TO [William Andrews Clark] / [Memorial Library].

Printed in 1955 by William Everson in an edition of 48 copies. Preliminary pages printed by Saul and Lillian Marks at the Plantin Press, Los Angeles. Bound by R. R. Donnelley & Sons Co. , Chicago.

Contains: "A Note on the Psalter of Pope Pius XII" by Everson.

The Psalter included the following note by Robert O. Schad:

Brother Antoninus, poet, printer and Dominican Lay Brother, whose artistry, idealism and
craftsmanship are embodied in these pages,
spent some three years on the printing of his
monumental edition of the Novum Psalterium
Pii XII. As the poet William Everson, he had
printed on his own Washington hand-press, two
volumes of his own poetry, A Privacy of
Speech and Tripych for the Living. Upon en-
tering the Dominican Order as a Lay Brother
in June, 1951, he set up his press in the College of St. Albert the Great in Oakland, California. It was there that he conceived the
idea of printing a folio edition of the new translation of the Psalter authorized by Pope Pius
XII.

For the five hundredth anniversary of the publication of the first Psalter, August 15, 1957,
Brother Antoninus aspired to print his own volume by the same methods used five centuries
ago by his great predecessors, Johann Fust
and Peter Schoeffer in Mainz. He began in
the autumn of 1951, calculating that it would
require six years to complete 48 copies of a
three-hundred page book.

As time passed and Brother Antoninus slowly
progressed with the Psalter, in such hours as
he could spare from his monastic life, his superiors in the Order felt increasingly that his
place was in the priesthood. For Brother Antoninus it was no small sacrifice to abandon
the book upon which he had lavished all the re-
sources of his craftsmanship, but the warm
approval of his superiors and his own deep inner conviction sustained him. In the Spring
of 1954, when he had finished seventy-two
pages, he closed his press and took up his
studies for the priesthood.

A number of advance subscriptions had been
taken, and Brother Antoninus was very con-
scious of his responsibility to those who had
given evidence of their faith in his work. He

turned to friend and fellow printer, Muir Dawson, for help. Mr. Dawson immediately went
to Oakland and took over the Psalter leaves,
proposing to publish them under the imprint of
Dawson's Book Shop.

From the first, Countess Doheny had been one
of the chief supporters of Brother Antoninus and
his Psalter. In this book, coming from her
own beloved California, she saw an extraordi-
nary manifestation of spirituality in printing.
Her profound religious faith, her many years
of experience as a collector in forming her
own library, and her devotion to fine printing,
joined to convince her that the Psalter, even
though incomplete, was worthy of preservation.

When Countess Doheny learned of Mr. Dawson's
plan, she asked if she might have the privilege
of sponsoring the publication and distributing
the forty-eight copies among important institu-
tions. Muir Dawson and his brother Glen most
unselfishly stood aside and relinquished their
project to her. Brother Antoninus was pre-
vailed upon to write an introductory note, and
this Countess Doheny had printed and bound
with the Psalter leaves in a manner befitting a
remarkable work of beauty, devotion, and craft-
manship.

B2   IN PROGRESS: ALDER GULCH
     AND OTHER POEMS   1961

In Progress / Alder Gulch and Other Poems / by bill
butler / illustrations / cliff robinson / introduction /
brother antoninus / [rule] / Published by / Haunted
Bookshop / & / Private Press / Berkeley, California

[20 pp.]. 22.4 x 14.7 cm. Light green printed wrappers, decorative rule and price. Woodcuts by Cliff
Robinson in black facing text.

Published in 1961 by Haunted Press Bookshop and Private Press.   Copy examined was signed by Brother Antoninus.

Contains: "Introduction" by Everson.

B3   CAWDOR / MEDEA   1970

Robinson Jeffers / A LONG POEM Cawdor / Medea
AFTER EURIPIDES / A NEW DIRECTIONS BOOK

xxx, 191 pp., 1 leaf.   19. 5 x 13. 3 cm.   Stiff paper
wrappers, printed.

Published by New Directions in 1970 as New Directions
Paperbook 293.   Published simultaneously in Canada by
McClellend & Stewart, Ltd.

Contains: "Introduction" by William Everson.

B4   CALIFORNIANS   1971

[in black:] Robinson Jeffers / [in red:] Californians /
[in black:] With An Introduction By / William Everson /
CAYUCOS BOOKS : 1971

xxvi pp., 163 pp., 1 leaf.   24 x 16 cm.   Brown vinyl
covered boards, stamped in gold: [cover] Robinson
Jeffers / CALIFORNIANS / [device]; [spine:] Californians / Robinson Jeffers / Cayucos.   Trump Medieval type, grayish brown endpapers.

Published in an edition of 500 copies by Cayucos Books
in October, 1971.   Fifty numbered copies are signed by
Everson.   Designed and printed by Graham Mackintosh,
bound by Filmer Bros.

Contains: "Introduction" by William Everson.

B5   WHERE THE OCEANS COVER US   1972

[in green:] Where The Oceans [in blue:] Cover Us /

poems by / MORTON MARCUS / CAPRA PRESS /
SANTA CRUZ / 1972

90 pp., 3 leaves. 23.6 x 16.4 cm. Decorative silk-
screen paper over boards: Where / The Oceans /
Cover Us / MORTON MARCUS / With a Foreword by
RICHARD HUGO and a Note by WILLIAM EVERSON;
green cloth covered spine: [in black:] WHERE THE
OCEANS COVER US / [in blue: design] / [in black:]
MORTON MARCUS. Illustration of the poet in brown
on title page. Blue endpapers.

Published by Capra Press, August, 1972, in an edition
of 100 copies, numbered and signed by the poet. Designed and printed by Noel Young, handbound by Earle
Gray.

Contains: "A Note" by William Everson.

B6   ROBINSON JEFFERS: MYTH, RITUAL, AND
     SYMBOL IN HIS NARRATIVE POEMS   1973

Robert J. Brophy / ROBINSON JEFFERS / Myth,
Ritual, And Symbol / in His Narrative Poems [design]
/ THE PRESS OF CASE WESTERN RESERVE UNIVER-
STIY / CLEVELAND & LONDON 1973

xviii, 321 pp., 2 blank leaves. 23.6 x 15.5 cm.
Green fabric covered boards, spine gold stamped:
BROPHY / [inset on brown: design] / ROBINSON /
JEFFERS / CASE / WESTERN / RESERVE. Light
green endpapers. Issued in dustjacket.

Published in 1973 by Case Western Reserve University
Press.

Contains: "Foreword" by William Everson.

B7   THE ALPINE CHRIST   1973

[in umber:] The / Alpine Christ / [in black: decorative
"&"] / [in umber:] Other Poems / ROBINSON JEFFERS

/ [in black:] With Commentary and Notes by WILLIAM
EVERSON / Cayucos Books [in umber: device] [in
black:] 1973.

xxix pp. , 200 pp. , 1 leaf. 26 x 18 cm. Off-white
cloth over boards, 1/3 leather spine in burgundy
stamped in gold: [rule] / THE / ALPINE / CHRIST /
[decorative "&"] / OTHER / POEMS / by / Robinson
/ Jeffers / [rule] / [rule] / CAYUCOS / BOOKS /
[rule]. First initial and half-titles decorative and in
umber. Gray endpapers, pages untrimmed.

Published in an edition of 250 copies numbered and
signed by William Everson by Peter Bartlett, Cayucos
Books, July, 1973. Designed and printed by Graham
Mackintosh at the Capra Press. Designated first printing in the colophon.

Contains: "Preface, " "Introduction, " "Afterword, " and
"Notes" by William Everson.

Note: Prospectus written by Everson. A trade edition
of this volume was published in 1974 at $12. 50.

B8   TRAGEDY HAS OBLIGATIONS   1973

[in black:] TRAGEDY / HAS / OBLIGATIONS / [in red:
swastika] / [in black:] ROBINSON / JEFFERS / THE
LIME KILN PRESS / 1973

[20 pp.].   40. 9 x 26. 9 cm.   Off-white cloth covered
boards, black spine gold stamped: ROBINSON JEFFERS
[device] TRAGEDY HAS OBLIGATIONS.   Woodcut in
black, decorative initials in red.   Numbered in red,
signed in black.   Weiss Roman and Italic types, Tovil
paper.   White endpapers, pages untrimmed.

Published by the Lime Kiln Press, the Library, University of California, Santa Cruz, in an edition of 200 copies
numbered and signed by Everson in 1973.   Printed by
Everson as a project for his course in printing.   Woodcut by Allison Clough.

Note: Photograph of holograph page of Jeffers' "Tragedy" tipped in following text.

Contains: "Afterword" by William Everson.

B9   BRIDES OF THE SOUTH WIND   1974

[in red:] Brides / of the / South Wind / [in black:]
Poems 1917 - 1922 / BY / [in red:] ROBINSON JEF-
FERS / [in black:] With Commentary and Notes by /
WILLIAM EVERSON / Cayucos Books / [in red:] 1974

xxxiii, 137 pp. , 1 blank leaf, 1 leaf.   24. 2 x 16. 3 cm.
Off-white cloth over boards; burgundy colored leather
spine, gold stamped: BRIDES / Of The / SOUTH /
WIND / [device] / Robinson Jeffers / [device] / Edited
By / William / Everson / [device] / CAYUCOS /
BOOKS.   Half-titles and section numbers in red.   Tan
endpapers.

Published in an edition of 285 numbered copies signed
by the poet in 1974 by Cayucos Books.   Designed by
Graham Mackintosh, printed by Noel Young, and bound
by Cardoza-James.

Contains: "Preface, " "Introduction, " "Afterword, " and
"Notes" by William Everson.

B10   GRANITE & CYPRESS   1975

[illustration] GRANITE & CYPRESS [device] ROBINSON
JEFFERS [device] RUBBINGS FROM THE ROCK /
POEMS GATHERED FROM HIS STONE-MASON YEARS
WHEN SUBMISSION / TO THE SPIRIT OF GRANITE IN
THE BUILDING OF HOUSE & TOWER & WALL / FO-
CUSED HIS IMAGINATION & GAVE MASSIVE PERMA-
NENCE TO HIS VERSE / THE LIME KILN PRESS [de-
vice] THE UNIVERSITY OF CALIFORNIA AT SANTA
CRUZ / ANNO DOMINI MCMLXXV

64 pp.   43. 2 x 31. 5 cm.   Bound in German Nature-

gewebe, spine open-laced with deerskin. Goudy Newstyle type, Castellar initials on Hayle paper. Silk
endpapers, pages untrimmed.

Published in an edition of 100 copies numbered and
signed by Everson by the Lime Kiln Press in 1975 at
$250.00. Title page woodcut by William Prochnow.

Contains: A selection of Jeffers' poems chosen by
Everson.

Note: Issued in slipcase of Monterey cypress; its window of granite is from Jeffers' stoneyard.

The following description, written by Everson, appeared
in the publisher's announcement for the book:

> The printers evolved a format conceived around
> the imagery of rock--not just the monuments
> the poet erected, but the substance itself, as
> sensory image, both visual and tactile, re-
> trieved from his contemplation of its nature,
> and memorialized in his verse as history's
> central archetype. Moreover, the long Jeffers
> line is shown here for the first time, released
> in broad format, thrusting the poems into a new
> dimension--their true dimension--in the read-
> er's mind.
>
> This extreme extension of line led to perhaps
> the most distinguishing feature of the book, in
> fact its central concept, one Everson had en-
> visioned for years but lacked the textual oppor-
> tunity to realize. Now the wide horizontal
> format adopted to accommodate Jeffers' extended
> line threw the problem of page proportion into
> the forefront, for with these dimensions the
> difference between recto and verso is magni-
> fied. It became apparent that to present each
> poem at its best only the recto, the righthand
> page, must be used. However, a uniformly
> blank page on the left, the verso, becomes
> tedious, then disturbing. It is like an un-
> sounded note in music: the ear craves cor-

respondence, and flinches when it is not there.
So with the eye and an open book: confronted
with endless blanks on the left, the recto sinks
like lead.

To overcome this deficiency, in processing
Granite & Cypress each sheet was skip fed.
The first pull was made on the naked tympan,
then the damped sheet of handmade paper,
placed over it, was run through the press.
This second pull, the true one, thus received
a reverse imprint of itself, offset from the
backup, so that in the finished book when the
reader turns the page the shadow of the previous poem in effect provides its own image to
enliven the verso, and the visual balance is
achieved. It is a feature which, as noted, constitutes the central original element in the design. And it is safe to say that in the whole
history of printing never before has this par-
ticular possibility been extended throughout a
substantive work to meet an actual aesthetic
need. This is justification enough. Its use
here further escapes preciosity in that the ab-
stract character of the receding image gives
point to the book's evocative subtitle: "Rubbings from the Rock." Like stone-rubbings
from his tower's lofty arch Jeffers' poems live
in yet another dimension.

Typographically the book is a synthesis of
disparate but sympathetic elements. It con-
sists of thirty-three leaves of English handmade paper, on the rectos of which Jeffers'
verse is handset in eighteen point Goudy Newstyle type, with the beautiful Castellar inline
initials used to establish the opening of each
poem. The leaves, printed damp on a double
crown Acorn handpress, present the graphic
image of each poem as it emerged in the
poet's developing awareness. In keeping with
the subject matter the format is stark, glyptic,
truly abrasive, recalling the feeling of per-
ceptive readers that Jeffers' lines truly hurt,

that to experience his language is to suffer his awful accessibility to the elements. The text, therefore, is unadorned save for a single title-page woodcut by William Prochnow.

Upon completion of the presswork the sheets were delivered to the Schuberth Bookbindery in San Francisco. There they were bound in rugged German Naturegewebe, and lined with Uwa paper from Japan. To complete the binding, and to maintain consonance with its origins, the spine is open-laced with deerskin rawhide from the California coast.

In the meantime, a slipcase was being conceived in Santa Cruz which again sets the work apart from any other edition of this time. Fashioned of Monterey Cypress, with a window of granite from Jeffers' stoneyard (rock drawn by the poet's own hands from the sea) it brings together the book's archetypal duality: the permanence of granite wrapped in the enduring presence of cypress. Contemporary in structure, the case is medieval in the quality of timelessness that informs it. It seems to have sprung from the past, emerged through a regrouping of primary energies out of that distant time when every book was rare, evincing from anonymous craftsmen the deepest responses of celebration and praise.

Readers will find here, then, four unprecedented features. In the book itself they will read together for the first time the nuclear body of poems which Jeffers wrote under the impact of stone, the transforming symbol of his creative emergence. They will see the long Jeffers line extended to its natural outreach, like the pulse and withdrawal of the tides to which he attributed his prosody. They will find a typography in which the implication of stone is carried to the ultimate, registering the wave-worn permanence of his mood and themes. And in the incomparable case which enshrines the whole they will possess the architectonic resolu-

tion of all these elements, memorializing the
achievement of a spirit intense but serene,
and the passionate instinct, immoderate and
fierce, by which he will always live.

B11   THE SIVAISTIC VISION   1975

JEFFERS: / The / SIVAISTIC / VISION / BILL
HOTCHKISS

254pp., 5 blank leaves.   24.7 x 15.5 cm.   Brown
fabric covered boards, stamped in gold: [cover]
JEFFERS: / THE SIVAISTIC VISION / Bill Hotchkiss;
[spine:] Hotchkiss / THE SIVAISTIC VISION / Blue
Oak.   White endpapers.   Issued in dustjacket.

Published in 1975 by Blue Oak Press, Auburn, California.

Contains: "Letter From William Everson."

C. CONTRIBUTIONS
TO PERIODICALS:
POETRY

1931

C1   "Gypsy Dance." The Caravan (Fresno State College), V, 1 (Dec. 1931) 40.

1934

C2   "Deserted Garden," "Compensation," "Autumn Song." The Caravan (Fresno State College), VIII, 1 (Nov. 1934) 16, 28, 31.

1935

C3   "October Tragedy," "Winter Plowing," "Poem" ["These Are the Ravens"], "First Winter Storm." The Caravan (Fresno State College), VIII, 2 (April 1935) 6, 16, 30, 34.

C4   "Do Not Brood for Long." Westward, IV, 8 (Aug. 1935) 13.

C5   "But There Was No Lament," "These Are the Ravens." The Ontario Herald, I, 15 (Aug. 16, 1935) 3.

C6   "Tor House (Carmel, July 31, 1935)." Carmel Pine Cone, XXXI, 38 (Sept. 20, 1935) 38.

C7   "Winter Plowing." Westward, IV, 10 (Oct. 1935) 25.

C8   "October Tragedy." Literature, III, 2 (Nov. /
      Dec. 1935) 2.

1936

C9   "Here the Rock Sleeps." Carmel Pine Cone,
      XXII, 8 (Feb. 21, 1936) 12.

C10   "The Flesh and the Bone " ["Fish-Eaters"].
      The Caravan (Fresno State College), IX, 1
      (April 1936) 44.

C11   "The Flesh and the Bone" ["Fish-Eaters"].
      Literary America, III, 6 (June 1936) 1181.

1937

C12   "The Eye Sees but the Heart" ["Fog"]. Carmel
      Pine Cone, XXIII, 2 (Jan. 8, 1937) 12.

C13   "The Watchers." Poetry, L, 3 (June 1937) 130-
      32.
          Two poems: "We in the Fields" and "Dust
      and the Glory" ["Attila"].

C14   "Sleep." The Saturday Review of Literature,
      XVI, 16 (Aug. 14, 1937) 5.

C15   "Who Worships the Sun" ["August"]. Carmel
      Pine Cone, XXIII, 34 (Aug. 20, 1937) 12.

1938

C16   "Poem" ["Orion"]. The Phoenix, I, 3 (autumn-
      winter 1938) 108-08.

1939

C17   "These Are the Ravens," "Do Not Brood for
      Long," "Fog Days," "First Winter Storm," "I
      Know It as the Sorrow." The Monthly Record
      (Connecticut State Prison), XLII, 3 (Oct. 1939)
      6, 8, 10.

C18   "To an Indian Hunting Posse," "Let It Be Told."
The Monthly Record (Connecticut State Prison),
XLIII, 1 (Nov. 1939) 32, 33.

C19   "We Walk the Young Earth; Conejo, California."
The Caravan (Fresno State College), XIII, 1
(Nov. 1939) 16.

1940

C20   "The Ruin." The Caravan (Fresno State College), XIII, 2 (Jan. 1940) 21.

C21   "Attila," "On the Anniversary of the Versailles
Peace." The Monthly Record (Connecticut State
Prison), XLIII, 3 (Jan. 1940) 23, 32.

C22   "The Sign." Poetry, LV, 5 (Feb. 1940), 243-
45.
     Submitted under the pseudonym "William
Herber."

C23   "Feast Day." Experimental Review, 2 (Nov.
1940) 32.

1943

C24   "Coast Thought." The Untide, I, 4 (Jan. 30,
1943).
     The Untide was a weekly newspaper published
by conscientious objectors interned at Camp Angel, Waldport, Oregon. Everson was interned
at Camp Angel from January, 1943, to early
1946.

C25   "Trifles." The Untide, I 5 (Feb. 6, 1943) 27.

C26   "Clouds." The Tide (Waldport, Ore.), II, 2
(Feb. 1943) 11.

C27   "War Elegy I (The Registration, October 16,
1940)" ["The Vow"]. The Untide, I, 6 (Feb.
13, 1943).

The War Elegy poems appeared as loose, un-
paged inserts.

C28   "War Elegy II (The Lottery, October 29, 1941)"
       ["Now in These Days"]. The Untide, I, 7 (Feb.
       20, 1943).
       The year, 1941, is a misprint for 1940.

C29   "War Elegy III" ["One Born of This Time"].
       The Untide, I, 8 (Feb. 28, 1943).

C30   "The Rancho" ["The Residual Years"]. The Tide
       (Waldport, Ore.), II, 3 (March 1943) 15.

C31   "War Elegy IV (The Prime Minister's Address,
       February, 1941)" ["The Unkillable Knowledge"].
       The Untide, I, 9 (March 5, 1943).

C32   "War Elegy V" ["A Winter Ascent"].   "War
       Elegy VI" ["Eastward the Armies"].   The Untide,
       I, 10 (March 13, 1943).

C33   "War Elegy VII" ["The Raid"].   The Untide, I,
       11 (March 20, 1943).

C34   "War Elegy VIII" ["Weeds"], "War Elegy IX"
       ["Night Scene"], "War Elegy X" ["Chronicle of
       Division," Part One, Poem XI].   The Untide, I,
       12 [March 27, 1943].

C35   "War Elegy I" ["The Vow"], "War Elegy II"
       ["Now in These Days"].   The Illiterati (Wyeth,
       Ore.), 1 (spring 1943) n.p.
       This issue was confiscated and destroyed by
       the U.S. Post Office.

C36   "Approach to the City" ["The Approach"].   The
       Tide (Waldport, Ore.), II, 4 ([April] 1943) [19].

C37   "Two War Elegies," "Do You Not Doubt."   The
       Iliterati (Wyeth, Ore.), [2] (summer 1943) n.p.
       "Two War Elegies": "One Born of This Time"
       ["War Elegy III"] and "(The Prime Minister's
       Address, February 1941)" ["War Elegy IV"].

C38   "War Elegy X (The Internment, Waldport, Oregon; January, 1943)" ["Chronicle of Division," Part One, Poem XI]. <u>The Tide</u> (Waldport, Ore.), II, 5 (July 1943) 18.

C39   "War Elegy VII" ["The Raid"], "War Elegy X (The Internment, Waldport, Oregon; January 1943)" ["Chronicle of Division," Part One, Poem XI]. <u>Circle</u>, I, 2 (1944), 12-13.

C40   "No, Not Ever, in No Time" ["The Impossible Choices"]. <u>The Compass</u>, I, 6 (spring 1944) 30-31.

C41   "Though Lying with Woman." <u>The Illiterati</u> (Waldport, Ore.), 3 (summer 1944) n.p.

C42   "I Call to Mind That Violent Man" ["The Outlaw"]. <u>The Compass</u>, II, 1-2 (summer-fall 1944) 9.

1945

C43   "Revolutionist." <u>The Illiterati</u> (Waldport, Ore.), 4 (summer 1945), n.p.

C44   "Yet Must the Man Marvel" ["Chronicle of Division," Part Two, Poem VII]. <u>The Compass</u>, II, 3-4 (1945), n.p.

1946

C45   "The Revolutionist," "The Outlaw." <u>Now</u> (London), 6 (summer 1946).

C46   "The Release" ["Chronicle of Division," Part Four, Poem VI]. <u>Circle</u>, 9 (1946), 38-39.

1947

C47   "If I Hide My Hand." <u>The Ark</u>, I, 1 (spring 1947) 38-39.

1948

C48   "The Flesh Waits On" [A Privacy of Speech, Poem IX]. The Illiterati (Pasadena, Calif.), 5 (1948) n. p.

1949

C49   "The Dusk," "The First Absence." Berkeley, 7 [1949] 7.

C50   "The Dance." Berkeley, 8 [1949] 7.

C51   "Time of Year: Three Poems of Autumn." The Pacific Spectator, III, 4 (autumn 1949) 384-85.
      The poems: "Odor of Autumn," "Yellow Weather," "Muscat."

C52   "The Carrousel." The Tiger's Eye, 9 (Oct. 1949) 102.

C53   "Triptych for the Living." The Catholic Worker, XVI, 7 (Dec. 1949) 3.
      The poems: "The Uncouth," "The Coming," "The Wise."

1950

C54   "In the Dream's Recess." The Catholic Worker, XVI, 9 (Feb. 1950) 8.

C55   "Making of the Cross." The Catholic Worker, XVII, 3 (Sept. 1950) 8.

C56   "At the Edge." The Catholic Worker, XVII, 5 (Nov. 1950) 5.

1951

C57   "Flight in the Desert." The Catholic Worker, XVII, 8 (Feb. 1951) 6.

C58   "Maurin House, Oakland" ["Hospice of the Word,"
       Section I].   The Catholic Worker, XVII, 11 (May
       1951) 8.

C59   "Maurin House, Oakland: Part II" ["Hospice of
       the Word," Section II].   The Catholic Worker,
       XVII, 3 (Oct. 1951) 3.

C60   "Advent."   Timbrel and Choir, I, 1 (winter
       1951) n. p.

                        1952

C61   "The Burning Book."   The Catholic Worker,
       XVIII, 6 (Jan. 1952) 5.

C62   "Full Summer" ["Past Solstice"].   The Catholic
       Worker, XVIII, 12 (July-Aug. 1952) 5.

       From this point on, Everson's contributions
           appeared under his religious name,
                   Brother Antoninus.

C63   "A Canticle to the Waterbirds."   The Catholic
       Worker, XVIII, 15 (Nov. 1952) 3.

                        1953

C64   "Massacre of the Holy Innocents."   The Catholic
       Worker, XVIII, 17 (Jan. 1953) 3.

C65   "A Jubilee" ["A Jubilee for St. Peter Martyr"].
       The Catholic Worker, XX, 1 (July-Aug. 1953) 2.

                        1954

C66   "Under a Keeping Spring."   Voices, 153 (Jan. -
       April 1954) 24-25.

                        1957

C67   "The South Coast," "A Penitential Psalm,"
       "Annul in Me My Manhood," "Out of the Ash."
       Evergreen Review, I, 2 [summer 1957] 17-20.

1958

C68   "A Siege of Silence." Chicago Review, XII, 3 (autumn 1958) 13.

C69   "The Encounter." Fresco, IX, 2 (winter 1958) 2.

C70   "A Canticle to the Christ in the Holy Eucharist." The Texas Quarterly, I, 4 (winter 1958) 121-23.

C71   "The Wise." Crossroads (Inglewood, Calif.), I, 6 (Dec. 1958) n. p.

1959

C72   "The Quittance of the Wound." Four Quarters, VIII, 2 (Jan. 1959) 18.

C73   "Rainy Easter." The Owl (University of Santa Clara), XLVI, 3 (spring 1959) 8-9.

C74   "A Savagery of Love." Fresco, IX, 3 (spring 1959) 2-9.

C75   "Zone of Death." Big Table, I, 2 (summer 1959) 66.

C76   "Jacob and the Angel." Jubilee, VII, 4 (Aug. 1959) [45-48].

1960

C77   "The Encounter." Fresco, X, 3 (summer 1960) 25.

C78   "A Canticle to the Great Mother of God." Jubilee, VIII, 8 (Dec. 1960) 16-20.

1961

C79   "The Word." Damascus Road, I, 1 [1961] 5-6.

C80   "Salmo Penitencial," "Cántico a Las Aves Acuáticas." Revista de la Universidad de Mexico, XV, 11 (July 1961) 8-9.
    Spanish translations, by Ernesto Cardenal, of "A Penitential Psalm" and "A Canticle to the Waterbirds."

1962

C81   "Salmo Penitencial," "Cántico a Las Aves Acuáticas." El Pez y La Serpiente (Managua, Nicaragua), 3 (March 1962) 55-59.
    Reprinted from C80.

C82   "In All These Acts." Poetry Northwest, III, 1 (spring 1962) 41-42.

C83   "God Germed in Raw Granite." The Commonweal, LXXVI, 12 (June 15, 1962) 300.

C84   "I Am Long Weaned." Choice [formerly Chicago Choice], 2 [summer 1962] 26.

C85   "The Song the Body Dreamed in the Spirit's Mad Behest." The Atlantic Monthly, CCX, 2 (Aug. 1962) 115.

C86   "All the Way to Heaven." The Critic, XXI, 1 (Aug.-Sept. 1962) 42-43.

C87   "The Hazards of Holiness." Ramparts, I, 2 (Sept. 1962) 47-54.
    Two poems: "The Beheading of John the Baptist" and "Judith and Holofernes."

C88   "Ucieczka no Pustynie," "Rzez Niewiniatek." Tvgodnik Powszechnv (Krakow, Poland), XVI, 32 (Sept. 12, 1962) 5.
    Polish translations, by Adriana Zielinskiego, of "The Flight in the Desert" and "The Massacre of the Holy Innocents."

1963

C89   "Annul in Me My Manhood." Way, XIX, 6 (July-Aug. 1963) 30-31.

C90   "A Canticle to the Waterbirds." Way, XIX, 8 (Oct. 1963) 32-35.

C91   "The Poet Is Dead." Ramparts, II, 3 (Christmas 1963) 85-90.

1965

C92   "Rosa Mystica." Sketchbook (spring 1965).
      Collected as "Prologue" in The Rose of Solitude.

1966

C93   "The Afterglow of the Rose." East Side Review, I, 1 (Jan.-Feb. 1966) 65.

C94   "The Birth, Selections from Triptych for the Living." The San Francisco Sunday Examiner and Chronicle (Dec. 25, 1966), "California Living," p. 7.
      Excerpts from "The Uncouth," "The Coming," and "The Wise."

1969

C95   "The Last Crusade." Evergreen Review, XIII, 66 (May 1969) 45-49.

C96   "Advent." Dialogue, II, 3 [1969] 52.

Except where otherwise noted,
from this point on, Everson's contributions
appeared under his given name.

1972

C97   "On Stinson Beach" ["Socket of Consequence"].

Lemmings (San Diego, Calif.), 2 [spring 1972]
n. p.

C98 "Goshawk." Quarry (College V, UC Santa
Cruz), 2 (autumn 1972) 68-69.

1973

C99 "Tide-turn." Maryland Poetry Review, 1 [1973]
n. p.
Five poems, printed here without titles:
"Ebb at Evening," "The Man-Fate," "Seed,"
"The Gauge," "The Gash." Printed under the
name, Brother Antoninus.

C100 "Goshawk." San Francisco Bay Guardian, 7,
24 (Oct., 1973) 16.

1974

C101 "Dark Waters." Sludge (Santa Cruz, Calif.)
[May 1974] n. p.

C102 "Original Sin," "Missa Defunctorum," "Missa
Sanctorem." Poetry Now, I, 3 [fall 1974] 2-3.

C103 "In the Fulness of Time." Bastard Angel, 3
(fall 1974) 52.

1976

C104 "The Tarantella Rose." New Catholic World,
CCXIX, 1309 (Jan.-Feb. 1976) 46.

C105 "Snowflake: The Death of Jeffers." Sierra
Journal (Rocklin, Calif.) [spring 1976] 15.

C106 "The Coming." Radix (Berkeley, Calif.) (Nov.
1976) n. p.

1940

D1   [Letter to the Editor].   Poetry, LVI, 2 (May
1940) 108-09.
    Everson explains his pseudonymous submission
of "The Sign" (cf. C22).

1943

D2   "Jazz. "   The Untide, II, 1 (April 18, 1943) 4-5.
    A reflective essay on jazz music, the piece was
printed anonymously.   (Cf. C24 regarding The Untide.)

D3   "The Dance. "   The Untide, II, 2 (May 2, 1943)
12-13.
    An essay on the development of the dance as
cultural expression, the piece was printed anonymously.

1944

D4   "The Fine Arts at Waldport. "   The Compass, II,
1-2 (summer-fall 1944) 20-27.
    An article describing the Fine Arts program,
of which Everson was the director, at Camp Angel
(Waldport, Oregon).

1946

D5   "Donne's The Apparition." The Explicator, IV, 8
      (June 1946) 56.

D6   "Letter from William Everson." Jazz Forum
      (East Mill, England), 2 (Sept. 1946) 10.
          A commentary on recordings of Bunk John-
      son, a jazz musician.

1949

D7   "The Poet and Poetry--A Symposium." The Oc-
      cidental (fall 1949) 39-46.
          Everson's contribution appears on pp. 41-42.

1950

D8   "Latter-Day Handpress: A Venture in Joy,
      Knowledge, and Tribulation." Quarterly News-
      Letter (The Book Club of California), XV, 2
      (spring 1950) 31-39.
          Everson recounts his development as a printer
      and the founding of his Equinox Press.

        From this point on, Everson's contributions
             appeared under his religious name,
                    Brother Antoninus.

1954

D9   "Printer as Contemplative." Quarterly News-
      Letter (The Book Club of California), XIX, 3
      (summer 1954) 51-60.
          Everson recounts his printing of the Novum
      Psalterium. The essay, with some revision, is
      included as "Printer" in the unpublished "Prodi-
      gious Thrust" (cf. 1B).

1957

D10   "Francis Thompson: One Great Taste of the
      Sky." The Monitor (Nov. 1, 1957).

Book review of The Man Has Wings: New
Poems and Plays by Francis Thompson, edited
by Terence L. Connolly, S. J.

1958

D11   "Brother Antoninus: Addendum." Supplement
(UCLA Librarian), (Nov. 14, 1958) 5-6.
Everson reflects upon the importance of the
public library to his development when he was
growing up in Selma, California.

D12   [Book Review]. The Monitor (Dec. 5, 1958).
Everson reviews The Word Is Love, a collection of poems by Sister M. Maura, S. S. N. D.

1959

D13   "Dionysius and the Beat Generation." Fresco,
IX, 4 (summer 1959) 2-8.
In this essay, Everson argues that the Beat
Movement embodies the re-emergence of Di-
onysius impulse in American Literature.

1960

D14   "Disclaimer." America, CII, 15 (Jan. 16, 1960)
435.
A brief letter from Everson, denying he had
called himself an "apostle to the squares," a
phrase attributed to him in the issue of Dec.
19-26, 1959, p. 369.

D15   "The Artist and Religious Life." The Benedictine
Review, XI, 3-4 (Sept.-Dec. 1960) 223-38.
An interview, conducted by Colman Barry,
O. S. B., the editor, and included as part of a
symposium, "The Catholic and Creativity." The
interview is heavily footnoted by Everson and
constitutes an important text.

1961

D16 "Symposium on the Teaching of Creative Writing." Four Quarters, X, 2 (Jan. 1961) 10-22.
Everson's contribution appears on pp. 21-22.

D17 "Correspondence." The Sewanee Review, LXIX, 2 (spring 1961) 351-53.
A letter to the editor, in which Everson comments on James Dickey's review of The Crooked Lines of God (cf. 2D). Dickey's rejoinder to the letter is printed here also.

D18 "Correspondence." The Sewanee Review, LXIX, 3 (summer 1961) 510-12.
A letter to the editor, in which Everson pursues points raised in the previous exchange with James Dickey (cf. D17). Dickey's rejoinder is also printed.

D19 "The Poet: An Essay by Brother Antoninus." Inscape, I, 3 (fall 1961) 31-33.
Printed transcript, with the poems omitted, of a reading given by Everson at Central Washington State College. Everson reflects upon the nature and role of the poet.

1962

D20 "A Tribute to Robinson Jeffers." The Critic, XX, 6 (June-July, 1962) 14-16.
Everson discusses his subjective relationship with the poetry of Jeffers in a eulogy to his "first mentor." With minor revisions, the essay was collected in Everson's Robinson Jeffers: Fragments of an Older Fury as "Not without Wisdom."

D21 "Pages from an Unpublished Autobiography." Ramparts, I, 2 (Sept. 1962) 55-64.
Three excerpts from Prodigious Thrust: "Friar," "Poet," and "Conversion." Prodigious Thrust, running to just over 500 pages in typescript, remains unpublished. (cf. 1B)

D22   "Our Modern Sensibility." The Commonweal,
       LXXVII, 5 (Oct. 26, 1962) 111-12.
       An essay on the poetic imagination, with
       particular reference to the poetry of Hart Crane.

D23   "Viridiana." Encounter (London), XIX, 6 (Dec.
       1962) 95.
       Everson comments on Buñuel's film Viridiana
       in a letter to the editor.

1963

D24   [Letter to Lawrence Clark Powell]. Quarterly
       News Letter (The Book Club of California),
       XXVIII, 2 (spring 1963) 31-32.
       The letter, included in "The Prospect before
       Us" (an address by Powell printed here), is
       dated March 18, 1947, and describes Everson's
       job as a janitor at the University of California
       Library, Berkeley. The address was collected
       in Powell's The Little Package, where the letter
       appears on p. 263.

D25   "A Conversation with Brother Antoninus." The
       Harvard Advocate, XCVII, 3 (spring-summer
       1963) 32-46.
       An interview conducted at Harvard by Albert
       Gelpi, Sidney Goldfarb, and Robert Dawson.
       The interview includes Everson's ideas on poetry
       and rhetoric, with reference to modern poetry,
       and also some significant autobiographical dis-
       cussion.

D26   "Dialogue on Holy Violence." Approach, 49
       (fall 1963) 40-44.
       Everson's contribution appears on pp. 43-44
       and is a rejoinder to Albert Fowler's review of
       The Hazards of Holiness, which is the other part
       of the "Dialogue." Everson discusses the role
       of violence in his religious poetry and in the
       spiritual life.

D27   [Review of The Beginning and the End]. Ram-
       parts, II, 3 (Christmas 1963) 95-96.

A review of a posthumous collection of poems by Robinson Jeffers. Somewhat expanded, the review was collected in Everson's Robinson Jeffers: Fragments of an Older Fury as "The Beauty of God."

D28 "The Tongs of Jeopardy." Season, I, 4 (winter 1963) 6-13.
This essay is a consideration of the assassination of President John F. Kennedy in terms of its archetypal character, in line with Jungian psychology, and its place in the American national psyche. Season is a Dominican journal published out of St. Albert's College, Oakland.

1964

D29 "The Tongs of Jeopardy." Ramparts, II, 5 (spring 1964) 3-9.
See D28.

D30 "Birth Control and Natural Law." Dialogue, IV, 8 (May 29, 1964).
Everson's contribution to this transcript of taped conference appears on pp. 7-8.

D31 "Flannery O'Connor--A Tribute." Esprit, VIII, 1 (winter 1964) 12-49.
Everson's contribution to a collection of letters eulogizing the late fiction writer appears on pp. 12-13.

1965

D32 "Death Has Pounced." Dominicana, L, 1 (spring 1965) 9-12.
An excerpt from the unpublished book The Tongs of Jeopardy, itself an expansion of the essay of that title (cf. D28).

1966

D33 "An Interview with Brother Antoninus." Renascence, XVIII, 3 (spring 1966) 137-45.

Conducted by Harry J. Cargas, the interview
deals largely with Everson's relationship with his
second wife, his poetry, and his spiritual experience.

1967

D34   "The Presence of the Poet." Windmill, 10 (Jan.
1967).
This printed transcript, edited by Everson,
bears the heading: "An Informal Discourse given
before the University of Oklahoma Philosophy
Club, Oct. 26, 1962."

D35   "Brother Antoninus." The Pacific Sun (May 26,
1967) 8-9.
This transcript of an interview conducted by
Adrianne Marcus. Copy examined bears the handwritten note: "It is the position of the poet that
the transcript as published does not accurately
represent what was uttered."

D36   "Woman." The New York Times Book Review
(Oct. 29, 1967) 54, 56.
A letter from Everson commenting on James
Wright's review of The Rose of Solitude, which
had appeared in the issue for Oct. 8, 1967.

1968

D37   "If I Speak Truth." Bay Podium, I, 1 (Jan.
1968).
Interview conducted by Jerry Burns. Somewhat on the casual side, the interview covers a
wide range of topics of contemporary interest.
The interview was published as a softcover book
(San Francisco: Goliards Press, 1968) under the
same title.

D38   "Brother Antoninus." The Tin Drum (Wesleyan
University) I, 4 (June 1968) 1, 4.
An interview conducted by Lawrence Clark
Powell and others. It is accompanied by a brief
article by Powell, "Brother Antoninus at Wesleyan."

D39   "Merton--Poet, Writer." The Catholic Voice
        (Dec. 18, 1968) 7.
            This news article on the death of Thomas
        Merton includes several statements by Everson
        on the significance of Merton and his work.

1969

D40   "Erotic Wedlock." Our Sunday Visitor, LDII, 2
        (May 11, 1969) 3.

        From this point on, Everson's contributions
            appeared under his given name.

1970

D41   "Earth Poetry." Sierra Club Bulletin, LV, 7
        (July 1970) 13-15.
            An abridged printing of the address later pub-
        lished as a folio pamphlet (cf. A34).

D42   "'Shut Not Your Doors to Me Proud Libraries'."
        California Librarian, XXXI, 4 (Oct. 1970) 226-
        27.
            An essay on the role of the library in the life
        and development of a poet.   The title is a line
        from Whitman.

1971

D43   "The Birth of a Poet: A Letter from Brother
        Antoninus." Anthology of Underground Poetry,
        13 [spring 1971] n. p.
            Everson used the title employed for this ap-
        pearance for the course of lectures he would give
        as poet in residence at the University of Cali-
        fornia, Santa Cruz.

D44   "William Everson Double Issue." Road Apple Re-
        view, III, 2-3 (summer-fall 1971).
            The issue features six lectures, edited for
        publication, given by Everson at the University of
        Wisconsin at Oshkosh: "Whitman, Emerson, and

the Frontier"; "San Francisco and Kerouac";
"I've Seen You a Thousand Times"; "The Poet
and His Words"; "The Poet as Priest"; and "The
Poet on His Poem: 'In All These Acts.'"

1972

D45   "Robinson Jeffers & the Mystic Call."   The Stain
       [April 1972] n. p.
          An essay on the relation between mysticism and
       poetry, with particular reference to Jeffers, this
       is excerpted from The Excesses of God, Ever-
       son's unpublished booklength study of Jeffers as
       a religious poet.   The Stain was a special literary
       edition of The Sundaze, Santa Cruz.

D46   "Continent's End (The Collected Poems of Robin-
       son Jeffers): A Proposal." Robinson Jeffers
       Newsletter, 31 (May 1972) 10-15.
          Everson presents his ideas on the arrangement
       and contents of a definitive collection of Jeffers'
       poetry.

1973

D47   "Astrological Note."   Robinson Jeffers Newslet-
       ter, 36 (Oct. 1973) 7-8.
          Everson discusses the uncertainty of Jeffers'
       time of birth.   The Everson Collection at the
       Bancroft Library contains a large amount of ma-
       terial for Everson's projected "The Sword in the
       Scales," which was to have been an astrological
       study of Jeffers.

1975

D48   "William Everson."   Right On, VI, 7 (March
       1975) 5, 11.
          An interview dealing with Everson's religious
       beliefs.   Right On is a far-left Christian journal
       published from Berkeley.

1976

D49   "A Poet's Belief." New Catholic World, CCXIX,
        1309 (Jan.-Feb. 1976) 44-46.
            The title under which the essay was submitted
        was "The Poet, the Totem, and the Animistic
        Christ." The essay was solicited for an issue
        devoted to poems and essays by Christian poets.

D50   "The Regional Incentive: Reflections on the
        Power of Place in Contemporary Literature."
        San Jose Studies, II, 3 (Nov. 1976) 51-59.

D51   "The Poem As Icon--Reflections on Printing As a
        Fine Art." Soundings, III, 2 (Dec. 1976) 7-21.

E. ANTHOLOGIES

E1   Poets of the Western Scene. Edited by Hans A.
Hoffman. San Leandro, Calif.: Greater West
Pub. Co., 1937.

        Contains: "Do Not Brood for Long."

E2   New Directions 9. Edited by James Laughlin.
Norfolk, Conn.: New Directions, 1946.

        Contains: "Note," "The Waldport Poems."

E3   One Hundred Modern Poems. Edited by Selden
Rodman. New York: Pellegrini and Cudahy, 1949.
Reprinted in paper as a "Mentor Book" (New York:
New American Library of World Literature, 1951).

        Contains: "The Raid."

E4   New Directions 12. Edited by James Laughlin.
Norfolk, Conn.: New Directions, 1950.

        Contains: "Triptych for the Living."

E5   Borestone Mountain Poetry Awards 1955. Stanford, Calif.: Stanford University Press, 1955.

        Contains: "Under a Keeping Spring."

E6   Helgon & Hetsporrar: Poesi fran Beat Generation
och San Franciscorenassansen. Edited by Reidar
Eknar. Stockholm, Sweden: Raben & Sjogren,
1960.

Contains: Swedish translations of "Out of the Ash" ("Ur Askan") and "Annul in Me My Manhood" (Upphar i mig min manlighet").

E7   The New American Poetry: 1945-1960. Edited by Donald M. Allen. New York: Grove Press, 1960.

Contains: "Advent," "A Canticle to the Waterbirds," and "The South Coast."

E8   The Californians: Writings of Their Past and Present (Vol. 2). Edited by Ursule Spider Erickson and Robert Pearshall. San Francisco: Hesperian House, 1961.

Contains: "Annul in Me My Manhood," "The South Coast," "Out of the Ash."

E9   Beat: Eine Anthologie. Edited by Karl O. Paetel and translated by Willi Anders. Hamburg, Germany: Rowholt, 1962.

Contains: German translations of "Annul in Me My Manhood" and "Zone of Death."

E10   Poetry Festival Commissioned Poems 1962. San Francisco: Poetry Center, San Francisco State College, 1962.

Contains: "The Poet Is Dead."

E11   Erotic Poetry: The Lyric, Ballads, Idyls and Epics of Love--Classical to Contemporary. Edited by William Cole. With a foreword by Stephen Spender. New York: Random House, 1963.

Contains: "The Presence," "March," "The Song the Body Dreamed in the Spirit's Mad Behest."

E12   Best Poems of 1962: Borestone Poetry Awards 1963. Vol. XV. Palo Alto, Calif.: Pacific Books, Publishers, 1963.

Contains: "God Germed in Raw Granite."

E13   A Selection of Contemporary Religious Poetry.
Compiled and introduced by Samuel Hazo. Glen
Rock, N.J.: Paulist Press, 1963.

Contains: "God Germed in Raw Granite."

E14   Antología de la Poesía Norteamericana. Translated by José C. Urtecho and Ernesto Cardenal.
Madrid, Spain: Aguilar, 1963.

Contains: Spanish translations of "A Penitential
Psalm," "A Canticle to the Waterbirds."

E15   Today's Poets: American and British Poetry
Since the 1930's. Edited by Chad Walsh. New
York: Charles Scribner's Sons, 1964.

Contains: "August," "The Stranger," "Hospice
of the Word," "A Canticle to the Christ in the
Holy Eucharist," "A Siege of Silence," "In All
These Acts."

E16   Modern Religious Poems: A Contemporary
Anthology. Edited by Jacob Trapp. New York:
Harper & Row, 1964.

Contains: "Jacob and the Angel."

E17   San Francisco Renaissancen: Ellve Moderne
Amerikanske Lyrikere. Edited by Erik Thygesen.
Copenhagen, Denmark: Sirus, 1964.

Contains: Danish translation of "A Canticle to
the Waterbirds."

E18   Poesia degli Ultimi Americani. Edited by
Fernanda Pivano. Milan, Italy: Feltrinel Edi-
tore, November 1964.

Contains: Translations of "Annul in Me My Manhood" and "Zone of Death."

E19   Nuestra Decada: La Cultura Contemporánea a
       Traves de Mel Textos (Revista de la Universidad
       de Mexico), Vol. 1. Mexico, D. F.: Universi-
       dad Nacional Autónoma de Mexico, 1964.

       Contains: Spanish translations of "A Penitential
       Psalm" and "A Canticle to the Waterbirds."

E20   The Tree and the Master: An Anthology of
       Literature on the Cross of Christ. Edited by
       Sister Mary Immaculate, C. S. C. With a preface
       by W. H. Auden. New York: Random House,
       1965.

       Contains: "The Making of the Cross."

E21   Studying Poetry: A Critical Anthology of English
       and American Poems. Edited by Karl Krober
       and John O. Lyons. New York: Harper & Row,
       1965.

       Contains: "A Canticle to the Waterbirds."

E22   Second Reading. Edited by Oscar Lewis. San
       Francisco: The Book Club of California, 1965.

       Contains: "Latter-Day Hand Press."

E23   1966 Peace Calendar & Appointment Book: Poems
       of War Resistance. New York: War Resisters
       League, 1966.

       Contains: "The Unkillable Knowledge."

E24   Harvard Advocate Centennial Anthology. Edited
       by Jonathan D. Culler. Cambridge, Mass.:
       Schenkman Pub. Co., 1966.

       Contains: "A Conversation With Brother An-
       toninus."

E25   The Cry of Rachel. Edited by Sr. Mary Immacu-
       late. New York: Random House, 1966.

Contains: "The Massacre of the Holy Innocents."

E26 Man's Search for Values. Edited by Thomas
Martin, Dorthy Chamberlin, and Irmgard Wieler.
Toronto, Canada: W. J. Gage, 1966.

Contains: "The Raid."

E27 Days of the Lord. Edited by William G. Storey.
New York: Herder & Herder, 1966. (Vols. 1
& 2.)

Contains: "Gethsemani."

E28 1967 Peace Calendar & Appointment Book. Compiled by Scott Bates. New York: War Resisters
League, 1967.

Contains: "Now in These Days," "One Born of
This Time."

E29 The New Modern Poetry: British and American
Poetry Since World War II. Edited and with an
Introduction by M. L. Rosenthal. New York:
Macmillan, 1967.

Contains: "I Am Long Weaned."

E30 Evergreen Review Reader. New York: Grove
Press, 1968.

Contains: "Annul in Me My Manhood."

E31 An Introduction to Literature. Edited by Mary
Rohrberger, Samuel H. Woods, Jr., and Bernard
F. Dukore. New York: Random House, 1968.

Contains: "August," "The Stranger."

E32 Patterns in Poetry: An Introductory Anthology.
Edited by Harry Brown and John Nulstead. Glenview, Ill.: Scott, Foresman and Co., 1968.

Contains: "The Stranger," "The Making of the Cross."

E33   Where Steel Winds Blow. Edited by Robert Cranie. New York: David McKay & Co., 1968.

Contains: "Attila."

E34   53 American Poets of Today. Edited with an Introduction and notes by Ruth Witt-Diamant and Rikutaro Fukuda. Tokyo: Kenkyusha, 1968.

Contains: "Muscat Pruning."

E35   Poems of War Resistance. Edited by Scott Bates. New York: Grossman Publishers, 1969.

Contains: "The Unkillable Knowledge" and an excerpt from "Now in These Days."

E36   Possibilities of Poetry. Selected and introduced by Richard Kostelanetz. New York: Dell Pub. Co., 1970.

Contains: "In Savage Wastes."

E37   A College Book of Verse. Edited by C. F. Main. Belmont, Calif.: Wadsworth Pub. Co., 1970.

Contains: "The Stranger."

E38   Interpretation Writer Reader Audience. Edited by Althea Smith Mattingly and Wilma Grimes. Belmont, Calif.: Wadsworth Pub. Co., 1970.

Contains: "Winter Plowing."

E39   I Love You All the Day It Is That Simple: Modern Marriage Poems. Edited by Philip Dacey and Gerald M. Knoll. St. Meinrad, Ind.: Abbey Press, 1970.

Contains: "The Quarrel."

E40   The Voice That Is Great Within Us.   Edited by
       Hayden Carruth.   New York: Bantam Books,
       1970.

       Contains: "The Flight in the Desert," "The
       Making of the Cross," "Zone of Death."

E41   Printing As a Performing Art.   Edited by Ruth
       Teiser and Catherine Harroun.   San Francisco:
       Book Club of California, 1970.

       Contains: "Interview."

E42   Two Ways of Seeing.   Edited by Wilson G.
       Pinney.   Photographs by Allen Say.   Boston:
       Little, Brown and Co., 1971.

       Contains: "Fish-Eaters."

E43   The San Francisco Poets.   Edited by David
       Meltzer.   New York: Ballantine Books, 1971.
       (Reprinted without poems as Golden Gate: Inter-
       views with Five San Francisco Poets, Berkeley:
       Wingbow Press, 1976.)

       Contains: Extensive interview, "October Tragedy,"
       "These Are The Ravens," "The Screed of the
       Flesh."

E44   Muse of Fire.   Edited by H. Edward Richardson
       and Frederick B. Shroyer.   New York: Alfred
       A. Knopf, 1971.

       Contains: "August," "The Stranger."

E45   Literature in America: The Modern Age.   Edited
       by Charles Kaplan.   New York: Free Press,
       1971.

       Contains: "A Canticle to the Waterbirds."

E46   Mark in Time: Portraits and Poetry / San Fran-
       cisco.   Edited by Nick Harvey.   Photographs by

Christa Fleischmann. San Francisco: Glide Publications, 1971.

Contains: "One Fragment for God. "

E47   What's in a Poem. Edited by John and Edith Wylander. Encino: Calif.: Dickinson Pub. Co., 1972.

Contains: "The Stranger. "

E48   Fine Frenzy: Enduring Themes in Poetry. Edited by Robert Baylor and Brenda Stokes. New York: McGraw-Hill Book Co., 1972.

Contains: "The Stranger. "

E49   Contemporary Poetry in America. Edited by Miller Williams. New York: Random House, 1973.

Contains: "San Joaquin," "Trifles," "The Stranger. "

E50   Regional Perspectives. Edited by Gordon Burke. Chicago: American Library Association, 1973.

Contains: "Archetype West. "

E51   Environmental Quality and Water Development. Edited by Charles R. Goldman, James McEvoy, III, and Peter Richerson. San Francisco: W. H. Freeman, 1973.

Contains: "The Hope We Have." Note: First compiled for the 1971 two-volume National Water Commission's study, Arlington, Va.

E52   The Norton Anthology of Modern Poetry. Edited by Richard Ellmann and Robert O'Clair. New York: W. W. Norton & Co., 1973.

Contains: "Year's End," "The Raid," "What Birds Were There. "

E53   The Poet in America: 1650 to the Present.
      Edited by Albert Gelpi.   Lexington, Mass.:
      D. C. Heath and Co., 1973.

      Contains: "We in the Fields," "August," "Bard,"
      "Lava Bed," "The Raid," "A Canticle to the Wa-
      terbirds," "The South Coast," "The Poet Is
      Dead," "In All These Acts," "The Song the Body
      Dreamed in the Spirit's Mad Behest," "The Rose
      of Solitude," "The Vision of Felicity."

E54   New Directions 28.   Edited by James Laughlin.
      Norfolk, Conn.: New Directions, 1974.

      Contains: "Tendril in the Mesh."

E55   Modern Poems.   Edited by Richard Ellmann and
      Robert O'Clair.   New York: W. W. Norton &
      Co., 1976.

      Contains: "Year's End," "The Raid."

F. EPHEMERA

F1   The Magnet. Vol. XXII. Selma, California:
Selma Union High School, 1929. High School
Yearbook includes photo of Everson (p. 29), letter
to the editor and poem (p. 81), and an ad for the
Everson Printery (p. 76).

F2   The Magnet. Vol. XXIII. Selma, California:
Selma Union High School, 1930. High School
Yearbook includes photo of Everson (p. 23), poems
(pp. 64, 65, 66, 67, 68, 70, 71, 75, 83), ad for
Everson Printery (p. 74), quip about Everson
(p. 82).

F3   The Magnet. Vol. XXIV. Selma, California:
Selma Union High School, 1931. High School
Yearbook contains photo of Everson (p. 16) and
photo of Everson as art editor (p. 30), poems (pp.
39, 70, 74, 76, 78, 80), illustrations by Everson
(pp. 50, 51, 67, 68, 69, 84).

F4   Fourteen Poems 1940-1941. Selma, California:
Broken Acres Press, 1943. This is an unpublished fragment. Type for this projected book was
set by James Atkisson and William Everson in
1942. Only the title page and leaves 9, 12, 13,
and 14 are extant, and each leaf in two copies
only. Everson retains one set of the five leaves.

F5   The Fine-Arts at Waldport. Waldport, Oregon:
Untide Press, 1943. An eight-page mimeographed
pamphlet written by Everson and published towards
the end of 1943. The pamphlet is a prospectus,

describing the School of Fine Arts, scheduled to open at Camp Angel in February of 1944. Conscientious objectors interned in camps all over the United States were invited to request transfers to Camp Angel if they were interested in becoming part of the Fine Arts program. Everson had been named director of the program.

F6   Vocation-Community. (Brother Service Committee Bulletin). Elgin, Ill.: Brethren CPS, 1945. Mimeographed pamphlet contains "Vocational art and community living," an essay by Everson.

F7   The Equinox Press. Berkeley, Calif.: Equinox Press, 1947. This broadside is principally an announcement by Everson of the establishment of his own private press. Printed by Everson, it is headed by a blockprint of a gryphon by Mary Fabilli. The broadside was printed in an edition of 500 copies and issued in the fall of 1947.

F8   Christmas card. 21.5 x 14.5 cm. Cover includes woodblock illustration of angel in green, text from John 1:14 in red and black, colophon in red. Eighty-five copies of this Christmas card were printed on the handpress and mailed "with the season's greetings by William and Mary Everson, THE EQUINOX PRESS, Christmas, 1948."

F9   God Writes Straight: The Anguish and the Peace of Brother Antoninus. An unbound, mimeographed 36-page survey of the poet's life, poetry, and ideas written by Everson under the pseudonym of Virginia Spanner. Its purpose was to provide a convenient source of information for press releases and other promotional activities in connection with Everson's readings. Circa 1959.

F10   Christmas card. 16.5 x 13.6 cm. Immaculate Heart College, Los Angeles, 1964. Cover text is lines from "Out of the Ash."

F11   The Dominican Brother. This is a Dominican

brochure on the life of the Brother, ca. 1966.
Only page of text is by Everson. Contains
photographs and captions.

F12   LSD No Substitute for Sin: Antoninus. Berkeley:
Oyez, 1966. Three-page offset press release
written by Everson in conjunction with a press
conference held Nov. 7, 1966.

F13   Brother Antoninus / Mystic of the Flesh. A
seven-page survey updating F5 through 1968.
Again written by Everson under "Virginia Spanner" pseudonym.

F14   "Melt down the Guns." This poem was printed
in the program distributed at the ceremonies in
San Francisco for the dedication of St. Francis
of the Guns, a statue by Benny Bufano. Program
also contains note by Mayor Joseph Alioto. June
6, 1969.

F15   Oyez Press Release, December 8, 1969. This
is a six-page typescript announcing the poet's
intention of leaving the Dominicans in order to
marry. Largely written by Everson, the press
release was apparently reproduced by Xerox photo-
copies. The first three pages deal with the deci-
sion itself, its circumstances, and the poet's personal comments. The remaining pages are a
summary of the poet's life and career. Approxi-
mately 25 copies.

F16   Wedding announcement. Announces Everson's
marriage to Susanna Rickson, 2 p.m., Sunday,
January 18, 1970, in Piedmont, Calif. 12.9 x
20.3 cm. Cover contains the words: Beauty is
momentary in the mind/ The fitful tracing of a
portal:/ But in the flesh it is immortal.

F17   "Birth of a Poet." This is a single sheet prospectus for a lecture course Everson presented
at Kresge College, University of California,
Santa Cruz for the 1971-72 academic year. The

course is subtitled, "An approach to ascesis as
applying to the vocation of poet." The prospectus
is hand-lettered in a variant of the Uncial style.
It appears to have been reproduced by off-set.
A photograph of the poet is reproduced on the
sheet.

F18   "The Original Manuscripts of William Everson
(Brother Antoninus). Part II: The Veritable
Years 1949-1969." (Oakland, Calif., ca. 1971.)
250 unnumbered pages in binder (mimeographed).
Nine copies produced by Robert Hawley as a de-
tailed description of the poet's archive (which
went to the Bancroft Library, University of California, Berkeley). Archive contained 3791 holograph pages, 9000 typewritten pages, 118 "fair
copies," 1900 carbon pages, 380 printed proof
pages, and 2452 pieces of correspondence.

Appendix 1

UNPUBLISHED MANUSCRIPTS

1A   "Introduction to In the Fictive Wish." This is an
      introduction written by Everson to an 87-page
      typescript collection of poetry written from the
      spring of 1946 to the end of 1948. This projected
      volume was never published as such, but when the
      complete pre-Catholic poetry was published in A31
      all the poetry collected here was included. The
      12-page introduction remains unpublished.

1B   Prodigious Thrust. Slightly over 500 pages in
      typescript, this prose work is the poet's auto-
      biography told in terms of his conversion to
      Catholicism. It was written from the fall of 1953
      to the summer of 1956. The book is divided into
      four parts. In addition, it contains a preface
      dated as of July 2, 1956, an epilogue written in
      the aftermath of Everson's unsuccessful attempt
      at the priesthood in the last half of 1954, and a
      brief poem entitled "Janua Coeli," which was
      published as A14. In addition to the prose text,
      part three incorporates the three poems of A11,
      and part four incorporates "The Falling of the
      Grain." The latter is a sequence of ten poems
      written in 1949, five of which remain unpublished.

1C   The Tongs of Jeopardy. During 1964, Everson
      expanded his essay of the same title into this
      book-length manuscript. The book is a considera-
      tion of President John F. Kennedy's assassination
      in terms of its archetypal character (in line with
      Jungian psychology) and its place in relation to

93

the American national psyche.

1D   Birth of a Poet: The Santa Cruz Meditations.
      Edited by Lee Bartlett. This long prose work
      consists of 24 "meditations" given by the poet at
      Kresge College, University of California, Santa
      Cruz during 1975. Part One, "The Presence of
      the Poet," deals with poetry and its relation to
      dream and myth in an attempt to define the voca-
      tion of the poet. Part Two, "The American
      Muse," contains six meditations on the situation
      of the poet in America. The final part of the
      book, "Archetype West," focuses on the poetry of
      region, with special reference to the West.

1E   Eros and Thanatos. This collects the following
      work into one volume: "The Poet Is Dead" (C91),
      "Missa Defunctorum" and "Missa Sanctorem"
      (C101), "The Tarantella Rose" (C102), and "Snow-
      flake" (C103), as well as others.

1F   The Mate-Flight of Eagles. Collection of poetry
      including "A Savagery of Love" and "The Cross
      Tore a Hole." With an Afterword by Allan
      Campo. Scheduled for publication by the Blue
      Oak Press (Auburn, California) in 1977.

1G   The Excesses of God: Robinson Jeffers As a
      Religious Figure. Everson has been working on
      this long prose study of Robinson Jeffers since
      1967. Originally an essay to have been included
      in A29, but withheld and since expanded. This
      work takes Rudolf Otto's Idea of the Holy and ap-
      plies it to Jeffers as a religious figure.

1H   The Veritable Years: Poems 1949-1966. Intended
      as a companion volume to A31, this book brings
      together all of the poet's religious poetry written
      under the name of Brother Antoninus. Everson is
      at present completing the editing of this volume,
      and hopes to finish the work sometime in the next
      two years.

Appendix 2

A CHECKLIST OF SELECTED CRITICISM

2A   BIBLIOGRAPHY (Arranged Chronologically)

Kherdian, David. Six Poets of the San Francisco
Renaissance: Portraits and Checklists. With an
Introduction by William Saroyan. Fresno, Calif.:
Giligia Press, 1967.

Meltzer, David, ed. The San Francisco Poets. New
    York: Ballantine Books, 1971. (See E43). (Re-
    issued in 1976 as Golden Gate, Berkeley: Wingbow
    Press.)

McDonald, John J. First Printings of American Authors.
    Detroit: Gale Publishing, 1975.

Lepper, Gary. 75 Postwar American Authors. Berke-
    ley: Serendipity Books, 1976.

2B   BOOKS, DISSERTATIONS, THESES, PARTS OF
      BOOKS (Arranged Chronologically)

Ethridge, James M. Contemporary Authors, IX-X.
    Detroit: Gale Research Co., 1964.

Mills, Ralph J. Contemporary American Poetry. New
    York: Random House, 1965.

Taylor, Jacqueline A. "Civilian Public Service in
    Waldport, Oregon, 1941-1945; The State Faces Re-
    ligion, Art, and Pacifism." Department of History,

University of Oregon, 1966.

Rizzo, Fred. "A Study of the Poetry of William Everson." Department of English, University of Oklahoma, 1966.

Campo, Allan. "Soul and the Search: Mysticism and
Its Approach in the Poetry of Brother Antoninus."
Department of English, Loyola University of Los
Angeles, June, 1966.

George, Sister Stephan Mary, O. P. "Brother Antoni-
nus: The Development of an American Mystical
Poet." Department of English, Boston College,
August, 1966.

Stafford, William E. The Achievement of Brother
Antoninus. Glenview, Ill.: Scott, Foresman and
Co., 1967.

Rosenthal, M. L. The New Poets: American and
British Poetry Since World War II. New York: Ox-
ford University Press, 1967.

Webster, Ronald F. "Mimesis of the Absolute: The
Revolt of Brother Antoninus." Department of English,
Gonzaga University, May, 1969.

Murphy, Rosalie, ed. Contemporary Poets of the English Language. With a Preface by C. Day Lewis.
New York: St. Martin's Press, 1970.

Charters, Samuel. Some Poems / Poets: Studies in
American Underground Poetry Since 1945. Berkeley,
Calif.: Oyez, 1971.

Lacey, Paul A. The Inner War: Forms and Themes
in Recent American Poetry. Philadelphia: Fortress
Press, 1972.

2C   PERIODICAL ARTICLES (Arranged Chronologically)

Mazzaro, Jerome. "Antoninus: Trihedral Poet."
    Fresco (winter, 1958), 4-10.

"The Beat Friar." Time (May 25, 1959), ("Religion").

"Antoninus Poetry to be Considered for Pulitzer Prize."
    The Varsity News (University of Detroit), Feb. 23,
    1960, 1.

Sullivan, Frank. "A Good Man ... and a Poet." The
    Loyola University Alumnus, XI, No. 5 (May 27,
    1960), 4.

McDonnell, Thomas P.   "The Poetry of Brother An-
    toninus." Spirit, XXVIII, No. 2 (May, 1961), 54-60.

Prochazka, Catherine. "Poetry--a Search." The Daily
    Tribune (Royal Oak, Mich.), Nov. 14, 1961.

Roehm, C. Stephen. "Brother Antoninus Everson, 'A
    Level Cup Near to Overflowing.'" Campus Detroiter
    (University of Detroit), III, No. 2 (Dec., 1961), 4,
    5, 14.

Hickey, John. "The Mystical Monk." The Boston
    Record-American and Sunday Advertiser, April 8,
    1962, "Pictorial Review," 4-5.

Hobbs, Lisa. "Creativity Is Born of Agony." San
    Francisco Examiner (Dec. 16, 1962), p. 22.

Willis, Michael S.   "Far-Out Approach to Spiritual
    Life." San Francisco Chronicle, Oct. 6, 1962.

Stiehl, Harry.   "Achievement in American Catholic
    Poetry." Ramparts, I, No. 3 (Nov., 1962), 26-38.

Krebs, A. V.   "Brother Antoninus: The 'Poet of In-
    surgence' Fulfills His Early Promise." Way:
    Catholic Viewpoints, XIX, No. 1 (Jan.-Feb., 1963),
    46-51.

McDonnell, Thomas P. "Poet from the West." The Commonweal, LXXVIII, No. 1 (March 29, 1963), 13-14.

Caro, Robert V., S.J. "Brother Antoninus: Engaging the Hidden God." Frontiers, V, No. 2 (spring, 1963), 71-75.

"Brother Antoninus: A Symposium." Dominicana: A Quarterly of Popular Theology, XLVIII, No. 1 (spring, 1963), 33-53.

Hazo, Samuel. "The Poet's Cult." The Commonweal, LXXIX, No. 5 (Oct. 25, 1963), 130-32.

Hailey, Jack. "The World of Brother Antoninus." Los Angeles Loyolan (March 8, 1965), 5.

McDonnell, Thomas P. "Brother Antoninus, Fastest Bard in the West." The Pilot (Boston), Nov. 13, 1965.

Carroll, Paul. "The American Poets in Their Skins 1950-1967." Choice, No. 5 (1967), 81-107.

Cargas, Harry. "The Love Poet." Marriage, LI (Feb., 1969), 44-48.

Stanger, Richard L. "All There Was Was a Man-- Struggling." The Christian Century, LXXXVI, 40 (Oct. 1, 1969), pp. 1247-49.

Rizzo, Fred. "Brother Antoninus: Vates of Radical Catholicism." The Denver Quarterly, III, No. 4 (winter, 1969), 18-38.

"Brother Antoninus to Marry." San Francisco Chronicle, Dec. 8, 1969, 1, 30.

Stanley, Don. "The Tale of a Triple Virgo." Pacific Sun, Oct. 14, 1970, 4-6.

Hoyem, Andrew. "The Poet as Printer." The Book

Club of California Quarterly News-Letter, XXXVII,
No. 1 (winter, 1971), 3-17.

Stein, Ruthe. "A Rebellious Man--From Monk to Marriage." San Francisco Chronicle, April 13, 1971, 18.

Childress, William. "William Everson." Poetry Now
(Eureka), I, 3 (fall, 1974), 21-22.

2D   SELECTED REVIEWS (Arranged Chronologically)

San Joaquin

Prussing, Jean. "Four Poets." Poetry, LVI, No. 4
(July, 1940), 220-22.

The Masculine Dead

Daiches, David. "Poetry for All Tastes." The New
Republic, CIX, No. 5 (Aug. 2, 1943), 149-50.

Algren, Nelson. "Magic and Melancholy." Poetry,
LXIII, No. 1 (Oct., 1943), 52-55.

X War Elegies

Harvey, Alan. "War Elegies." The Conscientious Ob-
jector, V, No. 8 (Aug., 1943), 5.

Bache, Kenneth. "War Elegies." The Compass, I,
No. 6 (spring, 1944), 38-39.

The Waldport Poems

Suchow, Ruth. "Review." The Compass, II, Nos. 1 &
2 (summer & fall, 1944), 40.

"Books Received." The Christian Century, Sept. 13,
1944, 1054.

Swallow, Alan. "A Review of Some Current Poetry."
The New Mexico Quarterly, XIV, No. 4 (winter,
1944), 481-84.

Drummond, Donald F. "Minority Report." Poetry,
LXV, No. 5 (Feb., 1945), 281-82.

War Elegies

Foff, Arthur. "Spring, Violence, Freud, Poetry."
San Francisco Chronicle, Jan. 21, 1945, 10.

Powers, J. F. "Review." Accent, V, No. 3 (spring,
1945), 190-91.

Dupee, F. W. "Verse Chronicle: Auden and Others."
The Nation, CLX, No. 21 (May 26, 1945), 605-06.

Van Duyn, Mona. "Conscience: Personal, Political,
Philosophical." Poetry, LXVI, No. 5 (Aug., 1945),
284-89.

Thurston, George. "Review." Circle, No. 5 (1945),
80.

Poems: MCMXLII

Webster, Harvey Curtis. "Goodness, Substance, Elo-
quence." Poetry, LXVIII, No. 4 (July, 1946), 227-
31.

Koch, Vivienne. "Poetry Chronicle." The Sewanee
Review, LIV, No. 4 (autumn, 1946), 699-716.

The Residual Years (1948)

Fiedler, Leslie A. "Some Uses and Failures of Feeling." Partisan Review, XV, No. 8 (Aug., 1948),
924-31.

Fitts, Dudley. "Subjective Weighing and Writhing."
The Saturday Review of Literature, XXXI, No. 47
(Nov. 20, 1948), 32.

Mowrer, Deane. The New Mexico Quarterly Review,
XVIII, No. 4 (winter, 1948), 462-66.

Parkinson, Thomas. "Some Recent Pacific Coast Poetry." The Pacific Spectator, IV, No. 3 (summer, 1950), 290-305.

Saul, George Brandon. "From Aridity to Affirmation." The Western Review, XV, No. 1 (autumn, 1950), 68-73.

The Crooked Lines of God

Deen, Rosemary. "Poetry of Conversion and the Religious Life." The Commonweal, LXXI, No. 24 (March 11, 1960), 656-57.

Rexroth, Kenneth. "A Struggle to Prepare for Vision." The New York Times Book Review, March 27, 1960, 10.

Deschner, Donald. "Hand Prints His Own Poetry." Los Angeles Herald & Express, April 25, 1960, A-12.

McDonnell, Thomas P. The Critic, XVIII, No. 5 (April-May, 1960), 28-29.

Mills, Ralph J. The New Mexico Quarterly Review, XXX, No. 2 (summer, 1960), 199-200.

Dickey, James. "The Suspect in Poetry, or Everyman as Detective." The Sewanee Review, LXVIII, No. 4 (autumn, 1960), 660-74.

Turco, Lewis. "Hitting It Lucky." Voices: A Journal of Poetry, No. 173 (Sept./Dec., 1960), 32-35.

Engels, John. "Two Religious Poets." Poetry, XCIV, No. 4 (Jan., 1962), 253-58.

The Hazards of Holiness

Rosenthal, M. L. "Pleasure and Anguish." The New York Times Book Review, LXVII, No. 36 (Sept. 9, 1962), 4.

Kenny, Herbert A. "The Hazards of Religious Poetry: A Shocking Book." The Catholic Reporter, Sept. 21, 1962.

Fiscalini, Janet. "Antoninus' Night." The Commonweal, LXXVII, No. 4 (Oct. 19, 1962), 100-01.

Burke, Herbert. "Review." Library Journal, LXXXVII, No. 19 (Nov. 1, 1962), 4025.

Schevill, James. "The Poets Speak from a Deep Personal Point of View." San Francisco Chronicle, Dec. 23, 1962, "This World," 21-2.

Creeley, Robert. "Think What's Got Away." Poetry, CII, No. 1 (April, 1963), 42-48.

Tusiani, Joseph. The Catholic World, CXCVII, No. 1177 (April, 1963), 61, 63.

Logan, John. "Poetry Shelf." The Critic, XXI, No. 5 (April-May, 1963), 85-6.

Korges, James. "James Dickey and Other Good Poets." The Minnesota Review, III, No. 4 (summer, 1963), 473-91.

Davidson, Peter. "New Poetry." The Atlantic Monthly, CCXII, No. 6 (Dec., 1963), 82-85.

Single Source

"Round Horseshoe Bend." The Times Literary Supplement (London), Aug. 18, 1966, 744.

Tillinghast, Richard. "Seven Poets." Poetry, CX, No. 4 (July, 1967), 258-66.

The Rose of Solitude

Davis, Douglas M. "Four Volumes Prove That Lyric Poetry Survives." National Observer, VI, No. 28 (July 10, 1967), 19.

Wright, James. "Personal Testament." The New York Times Book Review, Oct. 8, 1967, 16.

Kinsella, Thomas. "Orpheus Singing, Silence Blue," The Kenyon Review, XXIX, No. 5 (Nov., 1967), 704-12.

Cargas, Harry J. "Poetry by Brother Antoninus Celebrates Physical Love." St. Louis Review, Nov. 10, 1967, 18.

Murray, Michele. "Two of Six." The National Catholic Reporter, IV, No. 7 (Dec. 6, 1967), 13.

Dickey, William. "Intention and Accident." The Hudson Review, XX, No. 4 (winter, 1967-68), 687-98.

Gelpi, Albert J. "The Rose of Solitude." The Harvard Advocate, CII, No. 1 (March, 1968), 21-22.

Robinson Jeffers: Fragments of an Older Fury

Carpenter, Frederic I. "Review." American Literature, XL, No. 4 (Jan., 1969), 574-75.

Rizzo, Fred. "Review." The Denver Quarterly, IV, No. 1 (spring, 1969), 129-30.

McArdle, Phil. "Br. Antoninus & the Fascists." Los Angeles Loyolan, May 12, 1969, 4-5.

Brophy, Robert E. "Everson on Jeffers." Robinson Jeffers Newsletter, No. 38 (April, 1974), 2-4.

The Residual Years (1968)

Kirsch, Robert. "Brother Antoninus Poetry Published in Paperback." Los Angeles Times, Nov. 14, 1968.

Drew, Fraser. "Control and Penetration." Spirit, XXXV, No. 6 (Jan., 1969), 179-81.

"Poetry: Combatting Society with Surrealism." Time,

XCIII, No. 4 (Jan. 24, 1969), 72-76.

Waring, Walter W. Library Journal, XCIV, No. 3 (Feb. 1, 1969), 554.

Cohen, Robert. "Five Books." Poetry, CXV, No. 3 (Dec., 1969), 189-95.

Man-Fate

Frazier, Drew. "Review." Brushfire (University of Nevada), (spring, 1974).

Hahn, Claire. "Review." Commonweal, Vol. CII, No. 4 (May 9, 1975).

Matthias, John. "Songs & Conversations." Poetry, Vol. CXXVII, No. 2 (Nov., 1975).

Granite & Cypress

Blumenthal, Joseph. "Review." Fine Print, II, 2 (Apr., 1976), 26-27.

Archetype West

Vincent, Stephen. "Review." San Francisco Review of Books, II, 6 (Oct., 1976), 18-23.

Index 1

BOOKS, PAMPHLETS, BROADSIDES
BY WILLIAM EVERSON
(*Indicates a broadside)

Index 2

BOOKS WITH CONTRIBUTIONS
BY WILLIAM EVERSON

TITLES OF POEMS

TITLES OF PROSE